**IMAGINE THAT**

Licensed exclusively to Imagine That Publishing Ltd
Tide Mill Way, Woodbridge, Suffolk, IP12 1AP, UK
www.imaginethat.com
Copyright © 2017 Imagine That Group Ltd
All rights reserved
2 4 6 8 9 7 5 3 1
Manufactured in China

Written by Joshua George
Illustrated by Megan Higgins

ISBN 978-1-78700-388-0

A catalogue record for this book is available from the British Library

# The Biggest Bear
## in the Wood

Written by Joshua George

Illustrated by Megan Higgins

Look at me,

I'm feeling good,

I'm the biggest bear in the wood!

Look at me,

I'm feeling bad,

Those other bears made me feel sad!

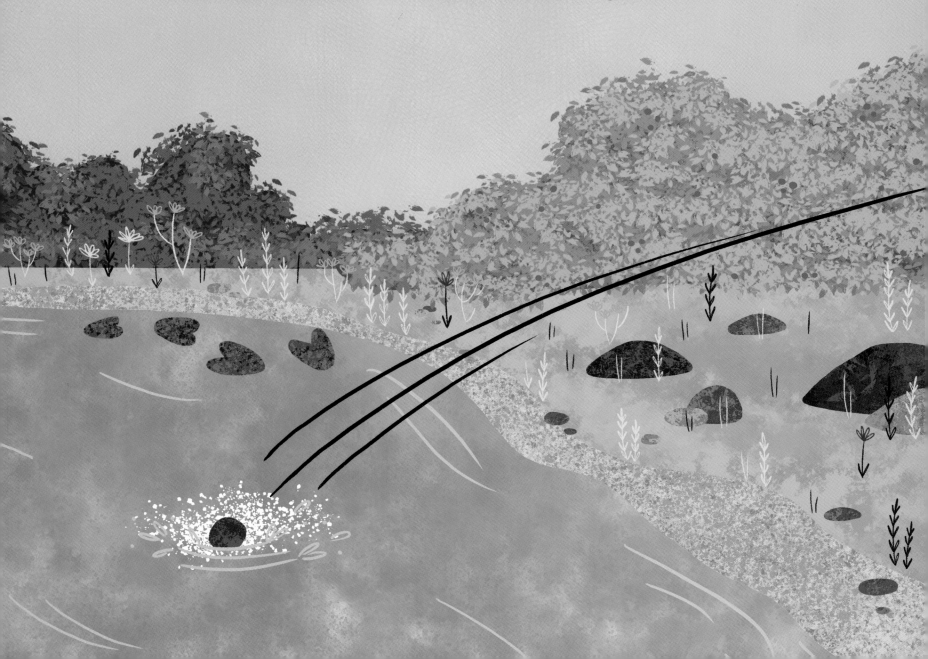

I've got small paws,

I've got small claws,

I'm feeling good, like a bear should!

I'm not the biggest bear of all,

But then again,

I'm not that small!

And that's not how the story ends ...

# Cardross
# The Village in Days gone by

## — an illustrated historical walk —
### by
### Arthur F. Jones

The old castle of Kilmahew

Dumbarton District Libraries
1985

## THE AUTHOR

ARTHUR F. JONES, M.A., A.L.A., F.S.A. (Scot.), was born at Cathcart, Glasgow, in 1946. After obtaining an honours degree in Philosophy at Glasgow University, he trained as a teacher and taught English at Clydebank High School until 1974. He then studied at Strathclyde University for a post-graduate Diploma in Librarianship, and was Reference and Local History Librarian with Dumbarton District Libraries from 1975 until 1983 when he became Librarian-in-Charge at Alexandria. From December 1984 he has been Librarian-in-Charge at Dumbarton Public Library. His wife is a native of Cardross and his interest in the history of the village dates from 1969.


DEDICATED TO
THE MEMORY OF
MY MOTHER
— Always there —


Front Cover Illustration: East end of Cardross in the early years of last century, from a drawing in sepia by
    William Havell (1782-1857)

Back Cover Illustration: East end of Cardross in the early years of this century.

Published by Dumbarton District Libraries,
Levenford House,
Helenslee Road,
Dumbarton,
Strathclyde.

c  Arthur F. Jones

I.S.B.N. 0 906927 17 X

Copying of some old photographs by Frank Melvin, photographer, Alexandria, and Messrs Mitchell & Averell, photographers, Dumbarton.
Modern photography by Arthur F. Jones.


Printed by J & J Robertson, 3 Poplar Road, Dumbarton

# PREFACE

In 1880 David Murray of Moore Park, Cardross, wrote a book entitled "Old Cardross", and referring to the agricultural and other improvements which had taken place throughout the preceding one hundred years, he concluded with the following remarks:

"The progress has been great, but is unabated, and I have little doubt that if, in 1980, an account of our times comes to be given, our ways and doings will be scanned with curiosity . . ."

"Let us hope, however, that Cardross may be found flourishing . . ."

In 1985 Cardross is indeed flourishing, and the changes which Dr. Murray predicted in general terms have certainly occurred. It is hoped that, while the present book has different aims from that of the celebrated Cardross antiquarian, it will nevertheless bring the story up to date and point the way towards the next hundred years.

It should be stressed that Dr. Murray concentrated on the early history of the parish as a whole, on changes in land ownership and management, and on agricultural improvement. He wrote in great detail about agriculture and about place names. The present book, however, is mainly about the village of Cardross which has, particularly within the last sixty years or so, become increasingly divorced, socially, from its agricultural periphery. This book does not, therefore, follow up the principal subject matters of its predecessor, and this might fairly be said to be the first account of the village as such.

While researching the book I have been privileged to read the various manuscripts and typescripts left by the late Ian McKinnon, one-time headmaster at Cardross School. For this I am indebted to his widow, Mrs Ethel McKinnon who still resides in the village. It became clear to me while reading this valuable material that Mr McKinnon had intended to produce a general history of the whole parish after the style of David Murray, and I have not been able to profit from his labours as much as I would have had I been writing with a much wider historical perspective in mind. However, perhaps a longer book dealing with the parish will appear at some later date; and whoever undertakes such a task will benefit greatly from Mr McKinnon's work.

In order to catch the flavour of village life over the last 130 years or so I have read all reports relating to Cardross village from 1851 and from 1880 in the "Lennox Herald" and "Helensburgh and Gareloch Times" newspapers respectively, together with more recent reports in the "County Reporter" and "Helensburgh Advertiser". This fairly onerous task has taken a number of years. The task of selecting from this material, appraising it critically, and drastically reducing what could have been written to a scale which could be encompassed within a small volume such as this, has been equally difficult and time-consuming. I hope that the information chosen will prove to be of interest.

The other printed and manuscript sources used for this book are too numerous to mention here; where they are thought to be of particular importance or relevance they are indicated in the text.

A great number of people have helped to make this book possible by supplying information verbally or contributing written material for consideration, or by lending old photographs — in some cases all three. Mr. Thomas Camlin of Rhu was of great assistance, as was Mr. Alex Walker of Church Avenue, Cardross, and Mr. Archibald McIntyre of Glenlee, Cardross — all gave most generously of their time, hospitality, and special knowledge in aid of the project. I should also like to record my gratitude to the following: Mrs. Christina Davis of Barrs Terrace; the late Mrs. Mary Sigsworth of Barrs Terrace; Miss Julia Colquhoun of Barrs Crescent; Mrs. Sheena Davie of Fairway; Mrs. McKillop of Barrs Road; the late Mrs. McLean of Cardross; Mr. Ronald Kinloch of Barrs Road; Miss Dorothy Ritchie of Church Avenue; The Rev. Andrew Scobie of the Manse, Cardross; Mrs. McKinlay of Keppoch; Miss Marie McWatt, late of Dumbarton District Libraries; and Mrs. McDonald, 5 Craig Ave., Tullichewan, Alexandria.

My thanks are also due to the members of Cardross Community Council which helped to fund this project (see Introduction). Their advice, and their patience in awaiting the outcome is much appreciated.

I would like also to make special mention of two people whose efforts on my behalf have been enormous. Firstly, Mr. James Adie of Dumbuie Avenue, Dumbarton (a native of Cardross) has been the source of much oral and written information, of photographs, and (equally important) of constant encouragement. His help has been invaluable. Secondly, Mr. William Jones, my father, of Colgrain Helensburgh, has helped me tremendously by dictating from an often semi-legible provisional manuscript text and by providing much practical advice and assistance.

Arthur F. Jones
July 1984

# INTRODUCTION

When the former Cardross Society noted that the District Library had begun to collect information on various localities with a view to producing local histories, it warmly supported this approach and at its final meeting, prior to the setting up of Community Councils, resolved unanimously that remaining funds be donated towards the costs of production of a Cardross book.

The Community Council wishes to record its appreciation of the great interest shown and the professional help given by the District Council Library staff in the production of this book, particularly the work of Arthur F. Jones. We commend the book to all residents of the village past and present.

*"In Cardros, quare Kyng Robert lay,*
*In lang seknes hys lattyr day"*
　　　　　　　— Wyntownis "Cronykil"

## CARDROSS VILLAGE: THE CHURCH, THE RAILWAY, AND THE MOTOR CAR

(N.B. Where the illustrations are referred to in the text, this is indicated by the abbreviation "ill." followed by the number of the illustration).

People sometimes refer to "the old and historic village of Cardross". Perhaps they have a vague idea that Robert the Bruce had something to do with the place; or maybe they are merely aware that there are a few old buildings in the vicinity. By any reasonable historical standard, however, the village of Cardross is not really particularly old at all.

It is a historical fact that King Robert the Bruce died at Cardross on the 7th of June, 1329, but this was at the "manerium de Cardross", the king's manor house, which stood near the River Leven and within the parish. This early parish, with different boundaries from the later one, lay to the west of the River Leven, ran north only as far as Pillanflatt, and west only to the Auchenfroe Burn; it extended also north westwards in irregular fashion as far as (and including) Glen Fruin and even to Loch Long. Most of the land on which the present-day village of Cardross stands was, in Bruce's time, within the then huge parish of Rosneath. Bruce's house (it was not a castle) stood not far from the site of the now demolished Mains of Cardross farmsteading, between the present Renton/Dumbarton road and the River Leven. The royal park may well have included the lands of Dalquhurn, Ardochbeg, Pillanflatt, and Kipperoch. Bruce kept a large boat on the River Leven and indulged himself in hunting and hawking until disease brought his final decline.

The village of Cardross cannot, therefore, claim any close connection with the former king other than is derived from the parish; and neither can Castlehill, now within the town of Dumbarton. Thus the housing scheme of Brucehill and the eccentric "Bruce's Stables" (the latter designed in the 18th century for a farm called Easter Hole, Foul Hole, or Braehead) are rather inappropriately named.

There was no village of Cardross in the days of King Robert. The land, under feudal control, would be worked by primitive farming methods; such people as there were would mostly be living in mere hovels scattered about the hillside. The parish church of Cardross stood with its glebe on the lands now called Levengrove (ill.1). The few remnants of this medieval structure can still be seen in Levengrove Park, Dumbarton, with memorials to the Dixons — 19th-century proprietors of the lands. It was a small oblong building with a tower at one end. The clachan of Kirkton of Cardross stood adjacent. If there was any village of Cardross in those days, this was it.

When the ecclesiastical authorities decided in the 1640s to redraw the boundaries of the parishes in the area, they were, unwittingly, taking the first step towards the creation of our village of Cardross. As a result of these changes the new parish of Cardross was extended westwards to Camiseskan, and so that the parish church would be more central, a small plain church was built in 1644 on a new site — where the familiar churchyard is today. As a result a clachan or hamlet grew up in the immediate vicinity and as far as Burnfoot. The usual agriculturally-related and other service trades such as blacksmithing and weaving provided occupations. In the years which followed a small settlement developed at Geilston and in the 18th century also some buildings were erected to the south of the main road (such as it was) opposite Cardross Park, accompaniments of the then fashionable improvement of estates. However, it is likely that even as late as 1800 there was little sense of there being one village called Cardross; but the basis for a village had been established and for its site we must thank the church in the form of the ecclesiastical authorities of the 17th century. That a larger church became necessary in 1826 was evidence that the settlements were growing. This growth was maintained, so that when the railway was constructed thirty years later there was no doubt that a station would be built there and named Cardross. The village complex, however, still consisted in 1858 of disparate settlements, and it was only as a result of the railway and the consequent feuing of land for the building of villas (mainly for Glasgow professional people who would be able to commute), that these settlements finally combined — from Craigend at the east to Geilston at the west.

Further Victorian and Edwardian housebuilding followed by an inter-war council estate on the lands of Barrs completed the village which the railway (with all its consequences) had made possible. Since the second world war and the advent of the motor car as a widely-used means of transport, more and more houses have been added to the older village to create a largish commuter settlement. Private housing schemes have recently been built on the lands of Kilmahew, Barrs, and Bainfield, and the built-up area of the village is now much larger. Many of the inhabitants have only been in the area for a short time, and the sense of village community identity exists only precariously. Indeed, people living in the newer schemes on the hillside have been heard to talk of walking "down to the village".

So the village of Cardross in the 1980s takes its situation from the Church, its physical unity from the railway, and its subsequent enlargement from the results of the widespread ownership and use of the motor car as a means of travelling to other places of work.

*Old adverts, date 1954*

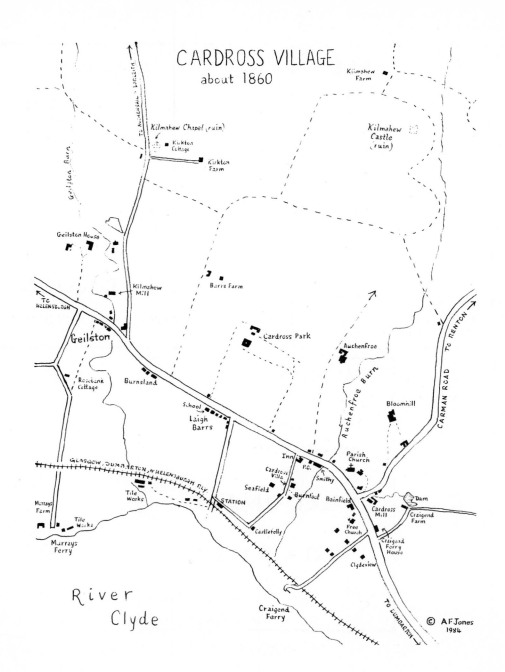

CARDROSS VILLAGE
about 1860

© A.F.Jones
1984

River
Clyde

10

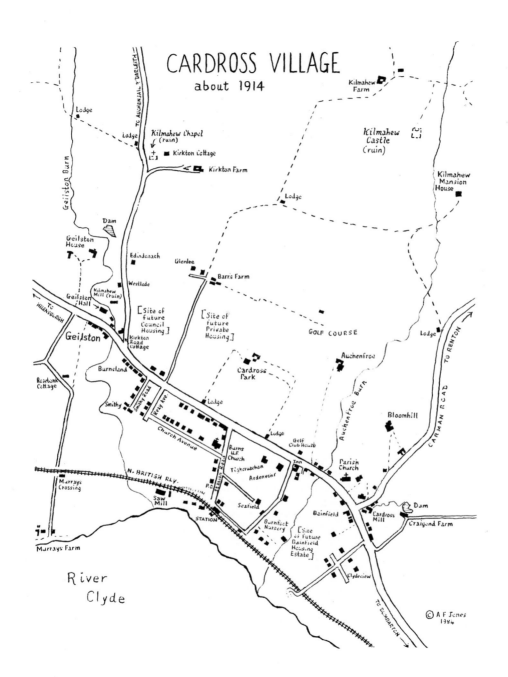

CARDROSS VILLAGE
about 1914

To AUCHENSAIL & DARLEITH

Kilmahew
Farm

Lodge

Lodge

Kilmahew Chapel
(ruin)

Kirkton Cottage

Kilmahew
Castle
(ruin)

Kirkton Farm

Kilmahew
Mansion
House

Geilston Burn

Lodge

Dam

Geilston
House

Edindonach

Glenlee

Barrs Farm

Kilmahew
Mill (ruin)

Westlade

Geilston
Hall

[Site of
future
Council
Housing]

[Site of
future
Private
Housing]

GOLF COURSE

Lodge

To HELENSBURGH

Geilston

Kirkton
Road
Cottage

Auchenfroe

TO RENTON

Burnsland

CARMAN ROAD

Rosebank
Cottage

Smithy

Smithy Road

Rly Ave.

Lodge

Cardross
Park

Bloomhill

Auchenfroe Burn

Church Avenue

Lodge

Golf
Club House

Burns
U.F. Church

Parish
Church

N. BRITISH RLY.

P.O.

Station Road

Tighcruachan

Ardenvohr

Inn

Murrays
Crossing

Saw
Mill

Seafield

STATION

Burnfoot
Nursery

Bainfield

Cardross
Mill

Dam

Craigend Farm

[Site
of future
Bainfield
Housing
Estate]

Murrays Farm

Clydeview

TO DUMBARTON

River
Clyde

© A F Jones
1984

11

# A HISTORICAL WALK THROUGH CARDROSS

Let us then take a historical walk through the village. Cardross is approached from the east by the A814 Dumbarton to Helensburgh road which, from its crossing of the River Leven at Dumbarton, has all the way been passing through the ancient parish of Cardross. Most of the land seen on both sides of the road was part of the old estate of Ardoch, once very extensive and associated with the Cunninghame Graham family and the Bontines before them. Ardoch House, residence of the Cunninghame Grahams, can be seen on the left at the foot of the Lee Brae. An older and larger residence once stood on the other side of the road near Ardochmore Farm.

A system of estate management controlled the agricultural and social affairs of Cardross until very recent times. Perhaps the most famous of all Cardross landowners was the author and adventurer Robert Bontine Cunninghame Graham (1852-1936) of Ardoch who celebrated his eightieth birthday in 1932 at the Queen's Hotel with a group of employees and Cardross friends. This also may have been the occasion of the transfer of the estate to Sir Angus Cunninghame Graham. Those in the photograph (ill. 2) are, back row, left to right: Mr. Sangster, solicitor; Hugh Mills Davie, butcher; ?; and James Barnes, stationmaster; middle row, left to right: Roddy McKenzie, Bruce's Stables; James Kinloch, farmer Ardochmore; John Clark, ex-Cardross policeman; David Adams, farmer Lea; James Gray, policeman; ?; Archibald McIntyre, Cardross Sawmills; John McIntyre, grocer; James Rosenburgh, joiner; George Rennie, farmer Westerhill; and James Lyle, plumber; front row, left to right: James Wilson, Ardoch Gardens; Peter Robertson, farmer Dalmuir; R.B. Cunninghame Graham; Lady Cunninghame Graham; Angus Cunninghame Graham; William Filshie; farmer Castlehill; John McKinstry, farmer Cardross Mill; and James McDonald, farmer Hawthornhill.

Only the easternmost part of the actual village of Cardross came within the old estate of Ardoch. This area is known as Craigend since it lies at the end of a cliff-like raised beach. "Clydeview" on the left is the first house at this end of the village, while on the right a farm road branches off to Craigend Farm and onwards to Walton Farm. Some of the villas on the left were amongst the first to be built in Cardross as a result of feuing which followed the coming of the railway in 1858.

The first house on the right stands immediately after Craigend Road. These semi-detached bungalows are approximately on the site of the old Craigend Ferry House, or Ferryman's Inn, where 150 years ago one could purchase oatcakes, skimmed milk, cheese and whisky. This two-storey building, latterly associated with the McDonald, McIndoe, and McGown families, once housed the Craigend ferryman. From the front you could see right down Ferry Road to the Clyde, and communication could be made from Port Glasgow opposite by a system of beacons. The Ferry Road was popularly known as the "Dummy Lane" — probably after deaf and dumb Joseph Ferrier who stayed at Craigend Cottage around the middle of last century.

A little along on the left lies the new Bainfield private housing estate built within the last ten years. On the right, after modern housing of different eras, stands the Cardross Mill filling station (at present used as a spare parts store), and behind, some remains of Cardross Mill itself which at one time had the double function of mill and farm. Some Cardross residents will remember the McKinstry family connection with these premises. Throughout the Victorian era the Ferrier family held the mill and farm here. In the old days the miller was an important figure in a rural community. The tenant farmers in the estate of which their farms formed a part had to bring their meal to be ground at the appropriate mill which itself was, of course, owned by the landlord and operated by one of his tenants. It is likely that this site for a mill is very ancient and the fact that the mill was called Cardross Mill (later also "Ardoch Mill") probably dates back to the time when the western boundary of the parish was at the Auchenfroe Burn.

Immediately after the Bainfield Estate road on the left stands the Swiss-style villa "Kirklands", presently the residence of Mr. Ian Muir. The villa was built at the beginning of this century for John Irving, engineering draughtsman with Denny & Co., Dumbarton, and local historian (having followed in the footsteps of his father Joseph Irving). The name by which the house is now known reminds us that on this site was built and opened in 1844, shortly after the "Disruption", the first Cardross Free Church (ill. 3). This extraordinarily modest and plain building was used for worship until the new building (now the Parish Church) was built at Station Road in 1872. The old church stood for a short time after that date and was used for Good Templar soirees and the like. On the right of the picture can be seen the old Free Church School, the first dominie of which (I am told) was Samuel Kelly, an Ulsterman, ancestor of the Cardross Kellys. This old building amazingly still exists in modified form as outhouses for "Kirklands". The villa behind "Kirklands" was at one time the Free Church manse, built in 1856.

The ministers of the Free Church in Cardross were:

(1) The Rev. John McMillan (1844-1858). He was deposed by the General Assembly of the Free Church of Scotland after charges of "Immorality", and refusing to accept this, he took his case to the civil courts, thus giving rise to the famous "Cardross Case" which turned on the right or otherwise of disestablished churches to be independent of the civil courts in matters ecclesiastical. The Rev. McMillan continued to reside in the manse for a number of years after his deposition. He was succeeded by,

(2) The Rev. Alexander Balmain Bruce, who left in 1868, and was later to write a biography of the shipbuilder William Denny and a history of the parish of Old Kilpatrick.

(3) The Rev. Thomas Crerar (1869-1879).

(4) The Rev. Robert Boag Watson (1879-1898) — a well-known mountaineer, conchologist and geologist.

(5) The Rev. Adam Mitchell Hunter, colleague and successor from 1897, and minister (1898-1921).

(6) The Rev. James W. Robertson (1922-1931). He was a keen supporter of the national union in 1928 between the United Free Church of Scotland and the established Church of Scotland, but his flock was opposed to the actual union of the congregations in Cardross at that stage.

(7) The Rev. David Ness (1932-1935).

(8) The Rev. Callum N. Miller Mackay 1937-  ; he was the last minister of the congregation before the union in 1945.

The number of adherents of the Free Church in Cardross was small in the early days owing it seems to the popularity of the parish minister, the Rev. William Dunn. By 1897 there were between 70 and 80 members, but by 1921 the larger number of between 170 and 180 is recorded.

In our next photograph (ill. 4) taken about 1930 we can see the main road at the east end of Cardross with the Carman road going off to the right. This photograph shows the original Bainfield named after the Misses Bain who were once liferentrixes of the property. They resided at Bainfield House, now called "The White House" (shown at the right of the picture), a building which dates from the eighteenth century — though the right hand extension (out of the picture) is much more recent. Robert Barr (died 1810), son of John Barr farmer and innkeeper at Sealandbank, stayed here as tenant at the beginning of last century. He was one of the old Cardross ferrymen, and it was his widow who shortly after 1810 built a new ferry house and inn across the road. This is the building shown at the far left of the photo. Today it is whitewashed and called simply "Bainfield". Mrs. Barr married secondly one, John Fraser, and the building was popularly referred to as "Fraser's Inn" until 1859 when he retired. This John Fraser, a native of Boleskine, Inverness-shire, was, incidentally, an ancestor of Sir Hugh Fraser of the House of Fraser retail chain. The male members of the Barr family were very famous oarsmen in their day.

There are several houses old and modern near the foot of Carman Road. On the right stands "Ladeside" (built 1883), until recently, and for many years the home of the Mitchell family. The late Arthur R. Mitchell, O.B.E., M.B.E., J.P., naval architect, was a member of the Board of Yarrow & Co., shipbuilders. The house is also notable as having been the last residence of a Cardross centenarian, Alexander Ewing. Born at Kirkton

13

(near Levengrove) in the parish of Cardross on 25th March 1801, he became for 28 years carrier between Glasgow and Dumbarton. He retired and eventually came to the village of Cardross (where his second cousin Alexander Ferrier was miller at Cardross Mill) and we see him (ill. 5) photographed at the age of 100 in 1901. He could remember the first ocean-going steamer "The Comet", the Peninsular War and the victory at Waterloo. He died at "Ladeside" on 16th December 1903.

Beyond "Ladeside" there was once a small cottage occupied, within living memory, by various families — e.g. McEachern, McConachie & Craig. The old Parish Church glebe is on your left near the bottom of Carman Road, and soon one reaches the entrance to the mansion house of "Bloomhill". It was built about 1838 for one, Alexander Ferrier. An earlier house called "Bloomhill", built for Andrew Edmonstone in the mid 1770s, stood a little to the north of the later site. It was pulled down by Alexander Ferrier when he built his new house. James Burns, later of Kilmahew, bought "Bloomhill" in 1848. It has had many occupants since, the best-remembered family being, perhaps, the Chrystals. Since shortly after the last war it has been a children's home. It is pictured (ill. 6).

## THE OLD PARISH CHURCH

As was mentioned in the introduction the Parish Church of Cardross was resited in 1644 when the boundaries of the parish were changed. A little further along the road from "The White House" we see the site which was chosen. The first church built in 1643-4 and illustrated (ill. 7) was a modest edifice which seated only 400 people — and it must have been pretty crammed at that. Old Alexander Ewing beforementioned remembered the old barn-like structure with the pulpit at the side wall. Opposite the pulpit were the gallery seats of the landed gentry whose say in the appointment of ministers was in these days considerable. Here sat the Dennistouns of Colgrain, the Smolletts, the Bontines of Ardoch, and the Napiers of Kilmahew. Apparently there was a small ante-room off the Dennistouns' pew which gave them the opportunity of an hour's repose between services! A small bell tower with weather vane can be seen in the illustration. The building underwent a complete and much-needed repair in 1775.

The second (and last) church on this site was a much-welcomed improvement on its predecessor. It was built in the Gothic style in 1826 to designs by George Dempster, architect in Greenock. The mason work was carried out by Robert Campbell, builder West Bridgend, and the contracted wright was William Brown also of West Bridgend near Dumbarton. It is interesting to note that it was constructed during the celebrated "year of the short corn", and not a drop of rain fell throughout the building process. While it was being built services were held, it seems, in a barn at Geilston. The new church was opened for worship on the last Sunday of April 1827 and could seat 800. The site is a splendid one with sheltering trees and an elevated position with fine views over the River Clyde. The photograph (ill. 8) taken sometime between the wars gives a good idea of the appearance of the church even if the darkness is a little exaggerated. The adjacent manse also illustrated is still the Parish Church Manse of Cardross. This building may have parts dating back as far as 1733; but it was either vastly altered or completely rebuilt for the Rev. William Dunn shortly after 1838. In 1869 plans were drawn up for improvements to church and manse. These were carried out between 1869 and 1870, and it was about that time that the old service road through the grounds of Bainfield was closed and a new approach made.

Among the internal alterations made at the time was the widening of the pews. "The great need of this we can testify from painful experience", wrote the "Dumbarton Herald" journalist in June 1870. "At present you sit in them bolt upright, and once in can't stretch a limb or lift one knee after another". He goes on with true "Dumbarton Herald" radicalism to comment that once you are "thus cribbed and cabined, you get a glimpse of a few favoured ones at a distance lolling in roomy quarters". This was "apt to breed thoughts of envy" which were "uncongenial to such a place".

James Honeyman, architect, was responsible for the alterations at this time though William Spence, architect in Glasgow, had also been consulted in 1869. James Donaldson of Keppoch was the benefactor. During the period of renovation services were held in the Drill Hall at Geilston.

In 1871 a beautiful east stained glass window was erected in the church to designs by Samuel Cottier of Cottier & Co., London. In the photograph (ill. 9) we can see the four sections each with a figure of one of the evangelists. One was presented by Mr. Campbell of Colgrain, one by Mr. Smollett of Bonhill, one by Mr. Dunlop of Gairbraid, and one by the members of the congregation. An organ was proposed in 1887 and was fitted by 1889, providing the first instrumental music heard in the Parish Church of Cardross. Until then singing had been led by a precentor or leader of psalmody. An advertisement of 1859 shows that the precentor at that time was paid £20 per annum. Archibald McColl of Ladeside was the first organist and choirmaster.

Concern was expressed about the state of the roof and the ventilation in 1897, and Messrs Boston, Menzies & Morton, architects in Greenock and Alexandria drew up plans for improvements. This gave rise to a great to-do over who was to pay. A repair fund was eventually instituted, however, the alterations were carried out, and the church reopened in July 1898. The roof was completely renewed. The old ceiling had been formed of circled ribs lathed and plastered; but this was replaced by a timber hammer-beam roof. The back gallery was redesigned and re-seated, and the whole church re-decorated.

Cardross Parish Church has been well blessed in its ministers over the years. There were two McAulays (unrelated) in the eighteenth century. The Rev. John McAulay was minister from 1774 to 1789. His son Zachary McAulay, celebrated philanthropist, spent his early years in Cardross, and was the father of the famous historian Lord McAulay. The Rev. Alexander McAulay was minister from 1791 to 1800 and the Rev. Archibald Wilson from 1801 to 1838.

The most notable minister in the nineteenth century, however, was the much-loved Rev. William Dunn who presided from 1838 to 1881. Born in Doune, Perthshire, in 1811, he is pictured (ill. 10) as he was in his prime. He devoted himself to his parish duties and did not involve himself much in public life or even in presbyterial affairs. A conscientious visitor, he also conducted his own Sunday School, young people's classes and devotional meetings. In 1845 he married Margaret Croll, a step-daughter of James Donaldson of Keppoch and when that laird died in 1875 Mr. Dunn went from the manse to reside at Keppoch House. He worked hard for the creation of the "quoad sacra" parishes of Renton and Dalreoch, helping to secure their endowment and disjunction, the whole parish having become unbalanced population-wise and unwieldy during his time as minister. The Rev. William Maxwell was appointed assistant in 1877 and took over in 1881 as assistant and successor, Mr. Dunn moving to Helensburgh where he died in 1885.

Mr. Maxwell's incumbency was also very lengthy. He was a minister in Cardross from 1877 till his death in 1931. He celebrated his jubilee in 1928 and he was one of the last ministers in Scotland to give up the celebration of the Fast Day before the sacrament of the Lord's Supper. This traditional practice was remembered by an old Rentonian Allan Bayne who in 1916 recalled walking over the hill to Cardross in 1848 to attend church with his mother. Many made the journey on foot, the women taking off boots and stockings till they reached the vicinity of the manse where they washed their feet at a well, and donned footwear again before entering church. Between the services some went to the shore and ate Abernethy biscuits sweetened by crushed imperial drops. Others went to the inn. Allan Bayne maintained that, contrary to the impression spread by Burns' "Holy Fair", drunkenness did not occur on the day of the sacrament.

This old custom was last observed in the summer of 1895. As has been said Mr. Maxwell died in 1931, so that during the long period of 93 years there were only two Parish ministers in Cardross. The ministers from Mr. Maxwell to the present day were and are: The Rev. Robert Andrew Agnew (1932-1936); The Rev. T.D. Stewart Brown (1937-1943) — last minister in the old church building; from here (in the present Parish Church building) — The Rev. Francis J.L. Maclauchlan (1946-1950); The Rev. Archibald A. Orrock (1950-

1964); The Rev. Andrew J. Scobie (1965- ). Mr. Scobie recently celebrated twenty years in Cardross and follows in the tradition of long-serving Cardross ministers.

The old churchyard of Cardross has many interesting monuments and is well worth a visit. Much can be learned here about the old Cardross families both wealthy and humble. The most popular surnames are an indication of the oldest families in the area, and among these are some which go as far back as there are records: Bain, Davie, Ferrier, Niven, and Traquair. There are still descendants of some of these families in the village today. Among other families still in the village and which have about 100 years connection or more with the area, and which are recorded on churchyard monuments are those of Camlin, Campbell, Cullen, Davis, Graham, Kelly, McArthur, McFarlane, McGown, McIntyre (both the Sawmill and the Drumhead Farm families), McPherson, Murray and Purdie.

Returning to consideration of the old Parish Church building, the last improvements made were in 1935-37 when new furnishings, a new chancel screen, chairs for minister and twelve elders, lectern and communion table were installed. On the night of 5th-6th May 1941, however, disaster struck during a German air raid on Clydeside when incendiary bombs destroyed the building, leaving only the shell. Commemorative services were held in the grounds in 1942 and 1943.

Moves towards the union of the congregations of the one-time Free Church and the Parish Church were naturally now accelerated, but the matter was rather prolonged and not without inevitable ill-feeling and sadness. Arrangements were finalised in 1945 and the Rev. Francis Maclauchlan soon after became minister of the united congregations. The "Burns" Church in Station Road was now Cardross Parish Church, though the possibility of the old church being rebuilt was not totally discounted at this stage, and in 1950 plans for a new church were actually considered. At the end of 1953, however, the congregation decided to proceed with plans for new church halls instead and to have the tower of the old church made safe and left standing as a memorial.

Another reminder, however, of the old days of worship on this site came with the sale in 1967, in London, of two Cardross communion cups made about 1700 by John Luke, a Glasgow silversmith. One is now in the Victoria and Albert Museum, London; the other in the Kelvingrove Museum and Art Gallery, Glasgow.

★ ★ ★ ★ ★ ★ ★ ★ ★ ★ ★ ★ ★ ★

Continuing westwards along the main street the grounds of Bloomhill with Shira Lodge are on the right and a variety of housing on the left. Soon the bridge over the Auchenfroe Burn is reached. Here is the western boundary of the ancient parish of Cardross as it was until the middle of the 17th century. The bridge is sometimes referred to as "Moore's Bridge" after Jean Watson, or Moore, a Cardross lady who left a legacy to the parish. The story goes that as a young woman resident in the lands of Keppoch towards the middle of the 17th century, she took a piece of salt beef from the laird's store and gave it to her indigent mother. Unknown to her this particular bit of beef had been specially put aside for the laird himself, and fearing retribution, she fled on a wet night but was forced to stop at the Auchenfroe Burn which was in spate. She is reported to have sworn there and then that if she were ever able she would have a bridge built there. She is said eventually to have reached Leith where she married a shipbroker named Moore, and later went with him to London where they acquired considerable wealth. She had the bridge erected at Auchenfroe as she had sworn and a tablet was placed on it with the pious inscription: "Not we, but God — Jean Watson". This can still be seen in the north parapet (ill. 13).

She also bequeathed, at the end of the 17th century, a sum of money to be used for the relief of the poor of the parish who resided between the Auchenfroe Burn and Keppoch. A fund was set up under a trust which was styled "The Trustees of Mrs Moore's Mortification". They invested the money by buying the lands of

Ballymenoch, the capital value of which, together with the annual rental, was of considerable benefit to the Cardross poor.

It has to be said that there is more than one variation on the theme of this story and a certain veneer of legend covers the basic historical facts, particularly concerning Mrs Moore herself. The Mortification, however, was very real. The fund was managed by the minister and Kirk Session of Cardross until 1860 when, the case having been taken to the Court of Session, pronouncement was finally made in favour of the Parish Council as the rightful authority for management. The Council had managed the affairs of the poor since the Poor Law Act of 1846. The Moore Mortification fund eventually passed to the County Council.

As you cross the Auchenfroe Bridge, notice the ancient little "Burnside Cottage" below street level (ills. 15 & 16). A few years ago the shape and angle of the roof were considerably altered. Standing by the roadside a little further on we can turn round and compare the present view looking back towards the ruin of the old church with the scene in our two early twentieth-century photographs (ill. 17 & back cover) and also with the early nineteenth century drawing in sepia by William Havell (1782-1857) — (front cover). In the drawing the earliest Cardross smithy can be seen behind the lady's panier. All the old houses shown in this picture disappeared in Victorian times.

The two Victorian cottage villas "Glenview" and "Westburn" on the right of the photographs are still standing. "Westburn" has, however, no longer a shop selling confections and teas as the sign shown on one would indicate. This shop was run until just after the last war by the McIntyre family and the building was, in fact, the first Cardross Post Office in the Victorian period.

Across the road an avenue leads from a lodge norwards to Auchenfroe House (ill. 18). This house was built, probably about 1820, for John McInnes, a West Indies merchant. James Burns of Kilmahew later acquired the property and it was leased by a number of families including John M. Martin of the Auchendennan family in Victorian period. Commander Wisnom of William Denny & Bros., Dumbarton, was there in the 1920s, and later, George Sloan. The Muir family is now resident. Until the 1870s the Auchenfroe Avenue continued to Darleith via Kilmahew.

Reverting to our original course westwards along the main road, we see the modern clubhouse of Cardross Golf Course with its lush fairways set out on part of the one-time Kilmahew estate. Golf first came to Cardross in 1895 when a six-hole course was laid out on another part of that estate (then owned by the Burns family) between the railway, Church Avenue, the main road, and Smithy Road. Where Reay Avenue now is, golf balls were once struck! Mrs Burns played the first ever golf shot in Cardross with a silver cleek in December 1895, and the Golf Club was formally instituted in January of the following year. In 1897 the first team match was played with Port Glasgow providing the opposition. The Cardross team which recorded a resounding victory (of course) was: Dr. Cullen, W.R. Sharp, John Scott, George Fraser, Archibald McArthur, Edgar Smith, Archibald McIntyre, John McIntyre, John Smith, and John J. McIntyre.

It was soon felt, however, that a longer course was required and a lease of part of the present site was acquired and the course designed by the celebrated golfer Willie Fernie. A match was arranged between Fernie and Ben Sayers for the opening of the new course on the 21st May 1904. Fernie went round the eighteen holes in 76, and Sayers in 77 (ill. 19). Work was soon started on the erection of a clubhouse — illustrated (ill. 20). Alexander McTurk of Helensburgh was the architect and Alexander McRae, joiner in Cardross, was the subcontractor. Upstairs there was a dining room and a smoking room with adjoining apartments for a resident caretaker, while downstairs were various club rooms and committee rooms. Some alterations were later made to the building. This clubhouse was yet another victim of the Cardross blitz of May 1941 and was sadly destroyed then. Our photograph (ill. 21) taken about 1920, shows the eighteenth green, the clubhouse, and behind, to the right, across the main road, Cardross Inn can be seen.

There have been, and still are, some notable golfers connected with Cardross and with Cardross Golf Club. Only a few can be mentioned here. William Davis (1908-1943), a native of the village who served an apprenticeship at Cardross Golf Club, brought honour to the area by winning the Scottish Professional Golf Championship at Inverness in 1939. He can be seen putting in the photograph (ill. 22). Of the Cardross Club professionals the longest serving was Simpson B. Wallace. An Ayrshire man, he came to Cardross in 1915 and remained a professional there until his death in 1955. He was a fine teacher and an early advocate of the change from hickory to steel shafted clubs. Cardross Golf Club today has two former Scottish Amateur Champions as members. Dumbarton's Charlie Green, the famous Scottish and British amateur internationalist, is in fact now a Cardross resident. He first won the Scottish championship in 1970. The other is Cardross man Keith Macintosh, a lawyer by profession, who won in 1979. There are also many fine lady golfers associated with the club, including Miss Hendry, Suzanne McMahon (nee Cadden), and Iris Keywood.

After the destruction of the clubhouse in 1941 Sir Maurice Denny allowed part of the mansion house of Ardenvohr across the road to be used, and from 1946 a number of wooden and Nissen huts served as temporary accommodation until the present clubhouse was built and opened in March 1956.

Let us return to the other side of the main road. The cottage villa "Glenview" stands on the site of the original Cardross smithy. Dr. McLachlan of Dumbarton, who compiled a series of articles on Cardross for the "Lennox Herald" in 1901 wrote of the old smithy and of John McCulloch, village blacksmith around the middle of last century:

> "It was, John remarked, a snod smithy, and well located, having the burn on the a'e side, and the inn on the ither. The burn was usefu' for drookin' the coal gum and laying the stoor, and at times for clapping a gizzened cart-wheel into; while the inn was at han' and handy for squaring accounts, washing the smoke out of one's mouth, and having a crack with customers in."

John McCulloch was, it seems, a typical old village smith — quite tall, broad shouldered, deep chested, brawny armed, and rosy cheeked, with his head a little bent from years of stooping over the anvil. He wore dark moleskin trousers held up by his leather brat which he frequently used as a handkerchief! He was highly skilled at horse-shoeing and plough-mounting, and could lay a coulter that did not contain a single flaw. The long hours and smithy stoor, and the sharpening of Sandy McPherson the sexton's picks, gave him quite a thirst, and many was the time he adjourned to the adjacent Cardross Inn to discuss the quality of the said picks and of spades and crowbars generally. No doubt they had the odd drink too! Meanwhile the smith's hammerman was looking after things until his boss returned.

The smithy itself had white-washed walls, a cranky door, broken windows, half shutters, a loosely-slated roof and a "crazy wooden smoke-ebonised ventilator". It had a half-folding big door where children used to climb to watch John McCulloch at work when a shoe forging was in progress, the bellows were blowing, and the sparks were flying.

Long before the end of the century the building was demolished and a new smithy built in the 1880s at the end of what became known as Smithy Road at the west end of the village.

The adjacent Cardross Inn, still standing, is a very old building (ill. 23) which was once also used as a farmhouse. The farm was known as Sealand Bank and the inn sometimes referred to as Sealand Bank Inn. During a large part of the Victorian period the inn was leased by the King family and was popularly called "King's Inn". The first member of this family to come to Cardross, John King, who hailed from Stewarton in Ayrshire, was in his young days a famous prize-winning ploughman and a keen curler; his wife displayed his many medals and trophies on occasions such as the annual dinners of the Agricultural Society and gatherings of the curling club.

As well as being used for the aforementioned purposes, the inn was the venue for an annual dinner laid on by the laird of Kilmahew when his farmer tenants paid their rents. Well into this century the courtyard of the inn was used for tethering horses during church services, and within living memory, the inn was a notable rendezvous for local farmers who spun many a yarn there, and gossiped endlessly. The inn was leased for many years this century by the McPherson family.

Let us now turn down Peel Street which runs from the main road to the railway where access to the shore is by a footbridge. On the right we first see the large Victorian Villa called "Ardenvohr", built about 1885 for W.B. Thomson, solicitor in Dumbarton. For a number of years this century this was the home of Sir Maurice Denny, Bart., of the firm of William Denny & Bros. Ltd., shipbuilders, Dumbarton. Further down on the right is the older villa called "Seafield" occupied for many years by a MacFarlane family who at one time had a grain merchant's business in Helensburgh and Glasgow.

On the left a variety of housing can be seen, some very recent. Just before Burnfoot, in which area there was once a thriving nursery which lasted well into this century (run for many years by the Morrison family and later by the Keywoods), a house called "Cardross Villa" once stood. The present building, "The Cottage", belongs to this century. "Ianmyo" is the next house on the left. It was once known as "Burnfoot Cottage", though a smaller house of that name now stands further down on the left, past "Seafield Cottage" which is on the right. At the bottom of the road a lane goes off to the left where the villas, each separately named, were long known as "Cosy Cottages". On the right a narrow lane leads to the station, with the railway on the left, and the gardens of modern houses on the right. At the corner of this lane stands the small house called "Tigh na Mara" which, within living memory, was occupied by the stationmasters Taylor and Barnes. Opposite, last century, stood an old house called "Castle Folly".

If we return to the main road and continue westwards, the grounds of Cardross Golf Course are on the right, while on the left a high wall stretches to Station Road. The next house on the left, after "Ardenvohr", is the modern "Bali Hi", erected for Mr. Ritchie the Cardross builder. On this site once stood an imposing square 15-room villa called "Tighcruachan" which had been built in 1880 for Donald McIntyre, an Argyllshire man, who had a meat merchant's business in Glasgow. Mr. McIntyre, who came to Cardross in 1876, took a great interest in the affairs of the village and was for many years a County Councillor for the area. He was of a benevolent disposition and took pleasure in helping the poor and in supporting recreational developments. For example, in 1901, he allowed the newly-formed Cardross Quoiting Club to use a field of his for practice and in that year he took a lease of McKinstry's Halls (near the top of Station Road) for the purpose of making the rooms available for reading and recreation. It was, it is worth recording, Donald McIntyre, who donated much of the statuary which graced the one-time Denny Institute in Dumbarton. He died in April 1906.

In February 1909 Donald McIntyre's former residence, "Tighcruachan", by this time owned by the MacFarlanes of "Seafield", was gutted by fire, only the blackened shell remaining. A stove in the billiard room at the top was thought to have overheated, setting fire to the wood. The Helensburgh Fire Brigade attended and later the Dumbarton Burgh Brigade, but, as was the case with so many Cardross fires in the old days, the absence of hydrants was a severe drawback. Water had to be pumped from the Auchenfroe Burn more than 300 yards away. The house was rebuilt and later known as "Borrowfield" which itself was destroyed in the Cardross Blitz in 1941. The old stables can still be seen beside the entrance to "Bali Hi".

On the right of the main road, after the golf course, is the entrance to the small estate known as Cardross Park. At the entrance gate once stood Cardross Park East Lodge (ill. 24), until about ten years ago. At the end of the driveway stands the huge mansion house of Cardross Park (ill. 25), built about 1810 for Thomas Yuille of the Darleith family, on the site of an even earlier house. The Edmondstones of Cardross Park were a well-known local family in the 18th century, and a family named Rodger occupied the house around the middle of last century. Towards the end of the century, a branch of the well-known MacBrayne shipping family was resident. Some local people will remember the times when, during the earlier part of this century, this was the home of Sir Archibald Denny, Bart., of William Denny & Bros., shipbuilders, Dumbarton. In our photograph

*Old adverts, date 1937.*

*Old advert, date 1937*

(ill. 26), one of Sir Archibald's motor cars, a Lanchester, can be seen at the door about 1906, with chauffeur William Adie sitting proudly in the driver's seat. The next photograph (ill. 27) shows Sir Archibald's domestic and other staff about 1910. Those identified are: back row, second from the left, Willie Purdie; in the middle, back row, Jimmy Campbell, assistant chauffeur; far right, William Adie, chauffeur; seated at left, front row, Mrs. Adie; and standing right, front row, Jessie Banks. We also have a photograph of the old coachman's house and garage (ill. 28). This picture was taken about 1938 looking from the stable door north eastwards. These buildings were demolished a few years ago, to make way for a new assessment centre.

In 1925 the mansion house itself was purchased by The Scottish Horse and Motormen's Association for use as a convalescent home for carters. In 1941 arrangements were being made for converting it for use as a children's hospital and home and since 1964 it has had the function of a remand home or assessment centre. In connection with this establishment new buildings were erected in 1977, to the east. The grounds to the south used to be in great demand for children's picnic parties, local sports, and so on.

If we return to the main road and walk westwards we reach on the right, the Cardross War Memorial, which reminds us that this village had its share of grief and suffering caused by the various wars of the last 200 years . . .

*Old advert, date 1912*

22

## CARDROSS IN TIMES OF WAR

Cardross people have been involved in the many national and international conflicts which have taken place over the centuries. In the very early part of the nineteenth century, during the Napoleonic period, when there was a massive recruitment into the regular army and the raising of local militia forces, some Cardross men must have enlisted. One principal land owner in the parish, Colonel Geils was abroad in India at this period serving the cause of empire.

The Volunteer movement became extremely popular from the middle of last century onwards. When we reach the Murrays Farm area in our historical walk mention will be made of the adjacent rifle range and an account of the local Volunteers will be given then; for although they assisted the regular army in war-time the movement was principally a source of leisure activity in Victorian times.

In the Crimean War (1853-1856), during the siege of Sebastopol (often regarded as the first instance of "modern" trench warfare), a young Cardross man Colin McIntyre wrote home to his father at Ardoch on the 27th October 1854 — "We have been ten days battering Sebastopol, but have hardly made any impression on it as it is all surrounded by batteries." Though near the scene of the conflict he asked for a newspaper to be sent on to him giving accounts of the victory of the Alma. He concluded by writing that he would send further news of the siege if he survived the taking of the city.

A public meeting was called in November 1854 and a committee formed to organise Cardross's contribution to the National Patriotic Fund. Colin Campbell of Colgrain presiding, called on everyone to "do his duty" by raising a fund for the maintenance and support of the widows and orphans of the soldiers and sailors who were sacrificing their lives in support of the balance of power in Europe. Liberal contributions were of course made mainly by those who could well afford them.

Cardross men also took part in the notorious and controversial Boer War (1899-1902). In March 1900 there was a special evening at Cardross Golf Club to honour Private John Kelly of the Black Watch who was wounded at Magersfontein. He had been greenkeeper before leaving to join the conflict in South Africa and was lucky to survive that terrible engagement, having been wounded in shoulder, side, and both legs, one leg being severely shattered. John Smith the Golf Club secretary and headmaster of Cardross School conducted a choir which sang martial choruses, and there were several solo performances. Private Kelly received a purse of sovereigns from the members of the club.

In 1901 Private Archibald Campbell, a well-known village painter and decorator, was also honoured with a presentation by the local people for his part in the Boer War. He received an inscribed gold badge, a pocket knife, and a purse of sovereigns, together with a volume of Burns' poems from the Literary Society. Later Private Campbell was carried shoulder-high through the village to the accompaniment of a brass band.

All this was of course little compared with the impact on the village of the first World War. War was declared on the 4th August 1914 and by the end of the month recruiting was well under way. There were also early appeals for recruits to the National Home Defence Reserve and many Cardross men were to be found on the muster roll. A County War Relief Fund was set up with district committees its various purposes being, to help the local Red Cross, the Soldiers and Sailors Family Association, and to give general relief from distress to the civilian population. The Cardross local committee was soon organising a great variety of fund-raising and other activities from knitting to special golf tournaments. Mrs Archibald McIntyre became secretary of the Cardross Relief Work Party, and by October 1914 they had already supplied over 2,000 articles for the Soldiers and Sailors Family Association, with the surplus being given to the Belgian children, the Red Cross, and so on. Concerts were soon arranged and the opportunity was usually taken to have some notable person there to appeal for further recruits for the forces. Children were involved in door-to-door collecting for the "penny-a-week" fund scheme.

Some people joined the local branch of the Citizens' Training Force set up to encourage recruiting and also to provide training for those ineligible for normal military service. Drill commenced in 1915 under the command of Mr. Hendry of Geilston House.

During Red Cross week in June 1917 a busy garden fete was held at Kilmahew (ills. 30 & 31), organised by Mrs. Claude Allan. There was a huge number of stalls and concerts were held in the house at intervals, with vocal and instrumental music, and dancing. This last part of the proceedings was organised by Mrs. Denny of Cardross Park. Mr. Fulton of Ardmore was in charge of outdoor games. Miss Maxwell, the Parish Church minister's daughter, was responsible for a variety of competitions. The Vale of Leven and Jamestown Band was there, and a Red Cross appeal speech was delivered by Sir George T. Beatson K.C.B. By the end of the week Cardross had raised over £1,000 — a lot of money in those days.

In August 1917 Cardross played host to wounded soldiers from various hospitals in the Glasgow area and provided a variety of entertainments.

A number of Belgian refugees were housed by Cardross families during the war, and in at least one case (as reported to me) the child became just like one of the family. The general appearance of the village, however, became rather dismal throughout those terrible four years largely as a result of the mandatory black cloth blinds and the blackened windows.

The worst horrors of the Great War were, however, not taking place on the home front but on the battle fields of Europe. Many were the Cardross men wounded in body and spirit by those horrific events, and 31 died in action or as a result of wounds or gassing. Their names appeared from time to time in the local press which gave such details as age, rank, and where the tragedy occurred. In some cases the press was able to furnish further information of family connections. Needless to say, each name and rank appears on the Cardross War Memorial.

Though we must never forget the sacrifice (in many cases the ultimate sacrifice) made by all, we may mention some Cardross men who were decorated for gallantry. Petty Officer J. Crook, Ladeside Cottage, was awarded the St. George's Cross for distinguished service during the Russian retreat from Galicia in 1917. Sergeant William Hutchison, Seaforth Highlanders, eldest son of William Hutchison coal merchant in Cardross, was awarded the Military Medal in 1918, and in the Geilston Hall that same year he was presented with the D.C.M. by Lord Inverclyde, and was also given a pocket book of notes by Campbell Martin of Drumhead on behalf of the people of Cardross. Major Robert Parlane Kinloch (ill. 32), headmaster of Cardross School, was a distinguished and much decorated soldier, having been awarded the Military Cross and the Croix-de-Guerre in 1918 for gallantry in France. Private James McKillop R.A.M.C., Australian Forces, son of the late Malcolm McKillop and of Mrs. McKillop, Murrays Farm, was awarded the Military Medal for gallantry in 1918. Angus McPherson, son of Dugald McPherson of Monarouidh Cottage, had a remarkable military career. At the age of 16 he joined the Scots Guards in 1907 and he was involved in the major conflict from the very beginning. His name is mentioned in connection with the many notorious scenes of carnage at Mons, the Marne, Aigne, Ypres, La Bassée, Armentieres, Loos, Vimy Bridge, St. Quentin, and Passchandall, during which he was thrice wounded. Field commissioned in 1915 he became major in 1918, having gained the D.C.M. (1915), the M.C. (1918), and the O.S.A. In November 1918, at Geilston Hall, he was presented with a gold watch and chain and a silver salver.

Many were the events which took place in the village in the aftermath of the war. Local clubs and societies were involved. For example, in 1919 there was a ladies' day at Cardross Golf Club on behalf of the Edinburgh Hospital for Blind Soldiers, and in the same year there was a children's peace celebration at Kilmahew with about 200 children present to enjoy sports, a ventriloquist, a conjuror, pipe band, and so on.

In 1919 a committee was set up to see about the erection of a war memorial in the village. This memorial, situated at the main road opposite the entrance to Station Road, was unveiled on Sunday 11th December 1921 by Sir Iain Colquhoun, Lord Lieutenant of the County, in the presence of a large gathering, (ill. 33). Many people were affected when the bugler sounded the last post. The Boys' Brigade under Captain Gemmell were present, as were the Girl Guides under Miss Allan of Kilmahew. There were memorial services afterwards in both the Parish Church and the U.F. Church. It should also be mentioned that another war memorial (listing all those who had served as well as those who had died), designed by William Vickers, sculptor in Glasgow, for the Parish Church, was unveiled by David Murray of Moore Park on Sunday 26th September 1920.

Nationally the social and spiritual effects of the so-called war-to-end-wars were enormous. The carnage in the trenches had been so horrendous that public questioning about whose interests were really involved in such international conflicts was possible on a scale never before practised (or allowed). After the war respect for wealth and power began to decline. These changes, however, worked themselves out more slowly in a rural village like Cardross than in the industrial areas. The number of women and men in domestic service certainly declined. Only the owners of the larger houses could afford to pay the higher wages now expected. In truth, a way of life which had existed in Cardross for untold generations (but particularly in the 18th and 19th centuries) amongst the so-called ruling classes with their tenantry and domestic servants, was fast disappearing.

The First World War did not of course end all wars. Britain declared war on Germany on the 3rd September 1939. A number of preparations had been made for defence throughout the country before that date. As early as March that year it was reported that Cardross had a big A.R.P. detachment with many volunteers for warden service. A siren was ordered for the village. Some still clung to the belief that war could be avoided. J. W. Arbuthnot, prospective National Unionist candidate for Dumbartonshire, spoke in March in the Geilston Hall and took the Chamberlain line that wh ile Hitler himself was a "kleptomaniac" the ordinary Germans did not want war. Chamberlain was the man to lead, he said . . .

When war did break out Cardross was soon involved, receiving many evacuee children and mothers from Clydebank. The local farmers had to furnish information about their crops and livestock to a special committee concerned with the control of food supply. A War Benevolent Fund was started in the County with Claud Allan of Kilmahew chairman of the committee. A Cardross War Work Party was set up and a fund-raising performance of "Cinderella" was staged by the children of the village under the leadership of Mrs Miller Mackay wife of the Burns Church minister. There were about sixty children taking part, and Cardross residents of today may be interested to read the names of those who played the principal parts: Cinderella — Annie Purdie; The Prince — David Hanning; Baron — Jim Kinloch; Baroness — Isobel McFarlane; The Sisters — Mary Thomson and Sheena McLeod; Fairy Godmother — Isabel McKinstry; Jester — Hugh Miller Mackay; Herald — Ian Bulloch. Others who took part in a well-staged tableau called "Rendezvous" were: Shepherdess — Patricia Denny; Shepherd — Ronald Kinloch; Cupid — Sheila McGowan; Gardener — Jim Sherriff.

The War Work Party produced socks, pullovers, scarves, mitts, etc., which were taken to Hartfield House in Dumbarton for distribution; while the local Red Cross were organising functions to raise money.

Between late 1940 and the spring of 1941, the war, in the form of a series of air raids, actually came to Cardross and to Clydeside in general. Areas with shipbuilding and heavy engineering were obviously the targets for the German pilots, but other places including Cardross suffered too. On the night of the 4th-5th May 1941 the flashes from exploding shells could be seen in the sky, and just before dawn, a battery sited beside Murrays Farm opened fire for the first time. A further raid on the night of 5th-6th May produced the worst effects on Cardross. When the raid was over, the "Lennox Herald" journalist wrote with deliberate vagueness:

"A village on Clydeside suffered severely in the raid, chiefly from incendiary bombs, though a number of high explosive bombs were also dropped."

The newspaper was not allowed to reveal that the village was Cardross until the issue of the 28th June. The alert had sounded about midnight on the 5th May, and soon the incendiaries, delayed action bombs, etc., began to have disastrous effects. The following properties were destroyed completely: Cardross Old Parish Church, and a cottage across the road (home of Mr. William Nicol); Cardross Golf Clubhouse; "The Cottage" (Mr. Hay's), and a smaller cottage (Mr. Keywood senior's), both in Peel Street; a cottage in Blairquhomrie Wood occupied by the aged Peter Wilson; Borrowfield House (Lady Denny's) — where Mr. Ritchie's house ("Bali Hi") now stands; "Glenlee" (McIntyre family, Sawmill) — only the shell remained, but it is now rebuilt; semi-detached villas (homes of Mr. Shanks and Mr. Vallance) on the main road between the Muirholm Hotel and Barrs Crescent; Hope Terrace opposite the Geilston Hall; an old cottage at the foot of the Murrays Road; Barrs Farm; Mollandhu Farmsteading and house.

Some notable properties which were damaged were: Ardenvohr House; Cardross Mill; the railway footbridge at the east end of the station; and Geilston Hall. In addition many more homes in the village suffered caved-in ceilings and blown-in windows, and there were many near misses. Several hundred craters were seen scattered throughout the village the following day.

The fire-fighting efforts of the villagers during the worst period were tremendous and only a limited amount of outside assistance was possible. Those near the Parish Church were just getting ready to tackle the blaze when another high explosive bomb fell through the roof and destroyed the main part of the building. The bell was seen crashing to the ground and rolling to the doorway. The church records were fortunately saved. Other bombs fell on the churchyard and the manse grounds, shrapnel causing damage to many of the gravestones.

Mercifully casualties were few. Only one person died "on the spot", but one or two elderly people did not survive much longer, having received a great shock as a result of the calamity in general or of the damage to their homes in particular. Younger people worked hard in the ensuing months to repair damage. The Weirs at Kirkton Farm, who had suffered the loss of glasshouses, a boilerhouse and various outbuildings, had within a year rebuilt the tomato houses and other buildings, cleared the debris, and filled in the surrounding craters.

When the disruption caused by these events had died down other activities were resumed. There was a fete at Kilmahew for War Weapons Week. There were many stalls and numerous competitions including "Bombing Berlin" and "Moustaching Hitler". Later Mrs Claud Allan, Kilmahew, received a thank-you letter from Mrs Churchill, 10 Downing Street, for work in the local Red Cross on behalf of the Aid to Russia Fund. The movement against wastage was well under way and Kirkton Road Cottage was used as the Cardross Salvage Depot. In 1942, for example, the W.V.S. and W.R.I. in Cardross held a salvage drive throughout the district. There was a Warship Week concert in the Geilston Hall in aid of the County's purchase of a destroyer. Innumerable dances took place to help the funds of the local Red Cross and the War Work Party.

In May 1943 the Cardross detachment of the Home Guard was fed in the open by the best cooks in the local W.R.I. Full field kitchen equipment was used. For breakfast, porridge, bacon, sausage and scrambled eggs with rolls and margarine were served, while dinner consisted of vegetable soup, stewed mince with beans, leeks, carrots, turnip, and golden wonders, followed by steamed treacle pudding and custard sauce. On the subject of the Cardross Home Guard it is worth recording that in 1944, Sergeant Ian C. Bridge of the 5th (Cardross) Platoon was presented with a testimonial by the Army Commander for the Area, for meritorious conduct.

Later in the year there was a fair at Geilston Hall during "Wings For Victory" week, with a children's procession in fancy dress and a baby show, and on the final day of the week the Cardross Bowling Club organised a parade through the village and a sports event. The ever active Eunice Murray, Moore Park, was chairman of the "Wings For Victory" week committee.

From November 1943 onwards, as a result of the Emergency Powers (Defence) Acts of 1939 and 1940, all unnecessary iron and steel railings, posts, chains, bollards, gates, styles, etc., were to be removed — and this must have altered the appearance of the village somewhat. It is worth recording also that in 1944 there was a very busy G.T.C. camp at Bloomhill.

Towards the end of the war the Cardross Platoon of the Home Guard was paraded by their Commander, Lieutenant Snodgrass, for the last time and was dismissed on 16th February 1945. They celebrated with a dance at the Geilston Hall. Arrangements at that time were being made by Eunice Murray and others for the welcome home to servicemen.

Finally it was over. The welcoming home took place at the Geilston Hall on 12th April 1946, and each received a gift. A musical programme was performed by Mrs Kinloch, Mrs Caldwell, and Mr. Donald MacSporran. There were Victory Day celebrations on 8th June, with a bus run for children to the three lochs and a children's sports competition. A garden party at Kilmahew marked the winding up of the Cardross War Work Party and the Penny-a-week Fund.

On the last Sunday of June, 1948, plaques with the names of the men of the district who had lost their lives in the 1939-45 war were unveiled at the War Memorial by Sir Iain Colquhoun, Bart., of Luss. Present along with several dignitaries were local ex-servicemen, members of the Women's Red Cross, the Boy Scouts and the Girl Guides. The ceremony ended with the sounding of the Last Post and the Reveille by a bugler of the Argyll and Sutherland Highlanders.

★ ★ ★ ★ ★ ★ ★ ★ ★ ★ ★ ★ ★ ★

Opposite the war memorial, Station Road runs from the Main Road to Cardross Railway Station. Starting at the top we see on the left a small landscaped area with a seat gifted to the village in 1932 by the Cardross branch of the S.W.R.I. This was at a period when there was a growing awareness in Cardross of the need for more sports and recreational activities and facilities. The seat was designed by Alexander N. Paterson, A.R.S.A., and is known locally as "the Rural seat".

Across the road, after the southern end of the tenement called "Villafield", an entrance once led to Rosenburgh the joiner's workshops and to McKinstry's bakery — a thriving establishment in the earlier part of this century. After this entrance stood, until a short time ago, a small cottage-like building (ill. 34). Originally a house, this building was used for a variety of purposes this century — mainly for small businesses. At the beginning of the century it was known as "McKinstry's Hall" or "The Baker's Hall". Some people will remember here the paint shop of Archibald Campbell, the slater's and plasterer's premises of R.D. McKean, the offices of Rosenburgh the joiner, and, more recently, premises of Robert Gray, monumental sculptor. Modern terraced cottages were built last year on this site. "Villafield" can be seen in the background of the photograph.

Further down, at the corner with Church Avenue, stands the present Cardross Parish Church (ill. 34). It has been the Parish Church since 1945. This pleasant and attractive church in the Gothic style was erected in 1871 and opened for worship on 14th January 1872 as the second Cardross Free Church, an earlier much smaller church having been (as has been mentioned) at the east end of the village where the house "Kirklands" now stands. The architect for the new building was John Burnet of Glasgow. The site chosen was a field which had a long time before been part of a farm known as Drumsaddoch which had stretched from near the present Kirkton Farmsteading on the hill right down to the shore. The entire field had to be cleared of whin bushes before building could commence.

Financial support to the project was given by the Burns family of Kilmahew, staunch supporters of the Free Church cause, and "The Burns Church" remained an alternative name until very recent times. The windows were of stained glass designed by Messrs W. & J. Keir, Bothwell Street Glasgow. The bells, five in number, came from the Gorbals Bell Foundry of J.C. Wilson, while the tower clock was furnished by Mr. Gilchrist of

Buchanan Street Glasgow. Some local or near local tradesmen involved in the building were: Mr. Barlas, mason, Alexandria; Messrs. Brown & Kennedy, joiners, Dumbarton; William Reid, plumber, Helensburgh; Mr. Logan, slater, Cardross.

In 1878 a fine "medallion" west window was introduced with stained glass by the Messrs. Keir of Glasgow, with depictions of Moses, Isaiah, Jeremiah, and St. Joseph, and below, the four evangelists. With the attractive symbolic ornamentation, the effect was after the style of the old glass in Metz Cathedral.

Singing in the Free Church had been led by a precentor since the "Disruption", but in 1898 an organ was gifted, and formally inaugurated on the 8th April. The church interior was renovated in 1899 by A. & J. Scott of Glasgow, the first alterations of that kind since the opening.

For a number of years the congregation continued to use the old church, some way distant, as the church halls; but eventually they were without accommodation, and an extension to the new church was built in 1903 consisting of a hall and vestry, formally inaugurated on 16th December. These additions were designed by Mr. D. Andrew, junior, of Glasgow, and blend well with the main church structure. Local tradesmen were involved, particularly A. McRae, joiner, Cardross, who had over-all charge of the working operation.

It is worth noting at this point that the one-time Cardross Literary Society used the hall for a number of years, organising lectures together with other social and cultural events.

In 1933 a garden fete was held at Kilmahew in aid of a further complete renovation of the church interior. A musical association was formed in 1939, and before and after this date congregational activities were many and varied. Since it became the Parish Church a similar spirit of enthusiasm and active involvement with the affairs of the village has marked congregational life under successive ministries, not least in the case of the present incumbent, the Rev. A.J. Scobie. He is a member of the Cardross Community Council, a keen supporter of youth activities within the church, and is noted for his support of the ecumenical cause.

An interesting addition was made to the church interior in 1981 when Miss Elizabeth C. Hendry of Geilston House gifted three embroidered panels in memory of her sister, Lorna Hendry. The Cardross Church Embroidered Panels (ill. 36) which are quite magnificent, are the work of Hannah Frew Paterson who took 2¼ years to complete the task.

Great attention was paid by the artist concerning choice of fabric textures and colours, and it is pleasing to note that some pieces of fabric were provided by members of the congregation. The background for each panel is of high quality cotton. A system of realistic, symbolic and ornamental designs was incorporated into each panel using a skilful blend of hand and machine embroidery, combined with crochet technique. It appears that no pattern was preconceived as a whole, but was rather the outcome of continuous creation.

The left hand panel portrays the vegetable world in day-time and is suggestive of an inland view from Cardross.

In the centre panel humanity is featured with mankind gathered under the cross.

The right hand panel depicts the mineral world in night-time and suggests a view across the river from Cardross.

Across the road from the church stand the church halls built in 1956 and formally consecrated on the 6th December that year by the Rt. Rev. R.F.V. Scott, D.D., then Moderator of the General Assembly of the Church of Scotland. These halls were a much welcomed addition to the amenities of the village. There is a main hall capable of seating 450 people and a lesser hall which can accommodate 150. Many are the functions which have been held in these halls since.

On the left, after the church halls, stands the bungalow "The Coppice" followed by a road leading to new houses which stretch in the direction of "Seafield House". After the grey-stone villa "Holmwood" there are

*The Church of Cardross at Kirkton of Levengrove in the 17th century, from a drawing by Captain Slezer* (*Text page* 7)

1

*R.B. Cunninghame Graham of Ardoch with friends and employees, Queen's Hotel, Helensburgh 1932* (*Text page* 12)

2

3

*The original Cardross Free Church (Text page 13)*

4

*The east end of Cardross at Bainfield ca 1930 (Text page 13)*

*Alexander Ewing (1801-1903) at Ladeside in 1901 (Text page 14)*

*Bloomhill House today (Text page 14)*

7

*Cardross Parish Church built in 1644 (Text page 14)*

8

*Cardross Parish Church built in 1826 (Text page 14)*

9

*Interior of Cardross Old Parish Church showing the east window erected in 1871*
*(Text page 15)*

32

34

*Rev. William Dunn, minister of Cardross from 1938 to 1881 (Text page 15)*

*Cardross Old Parish Church ruin as it is today*

*Carved face, one of a pair, at the south doorway, Cardross Old Parish Church*

13

14

*Commemorative plaque and shield on the Bridge at Auchenfroe (Text page 16)*

36

*Burnside Cottage before and after recent alterations (Text page 17)*

Parish Church, Cardross.

17

*The main road, Cardross, looking east from Glenview towards the Church early this century (Text page 17)*

18

*Auchenfroe House today* (*Text page 17*)

*Fernie & Sayers playing the opening match on the new Cardross Golf Course*
(*Text page 17*)

19

*Cardross Golf Clubhouse about 1920 (Text page 17)*

20

21

*Cardross Golf Clubhouse and the last green about 1920* (*Text page 17*)

*Cardross man, William Davis, who won the Scottish Professional Championship in 1939 (Text page 18)*

23

*Cardross Inn today* (*Text page 18*)

24

*Cardross Park East Lodge about 1927 (Text page 19)*

25

*Cardross Park today (Text page 19)*

26

*Sir Archibald Denny's Lanchester at Cardross Park with chauffeur William Adie at the wheel about 1906 (Text page 22)*

27

*Cardross Park domestic staff about 1910 (Text page 22)*

*Coachman's House, Garage, Cardross Park, about 1938 (Text page 22)*

28

*Cardross Park West Lodge about 1938 (Text page 78)*

29

45

30

31

*War-time fête at Kilmahew 1917 (Text page 24)*

46

*Major Robert Parlane Kinloch, M.C., C. de G., M.A., F.E.I.S. (Text page 24)*

*Cardross War Memorial 1921 (Text page 24)*

*The one-time "McKinstry's Hall" in 1979 (Text page 27)*

35

*Cardross Parish Church today (Text page 27)*

36

*Central section of Cardross Parish Church embroidered panels (Text page 28)*

*Station Road at the beginning of this century (Text page 71)*

37

38

*Cardross Railway Station about 1913* (*Text page 71*)

39

*Cardross Railway staff about 1913* (*Text page 71*)

50

## 40

*Cardross Railway staff pictured at the signal box 1923 (Text page 71)*

41

CARDROSS SHORE.

*Cardross Shore at the beginning of this century* (*Text page 72*)

52

42

43

*Workforce of John McIntyre & Son, Sawmillers, about 1920 (Text pages 73-74)*

53

44

*Premises of John McIntyre & Son, Sawmillers, about 1947 (Text page 74)*

45

54

*The members of Cardross Rovers F.C. winners of the Lochside Cup in 1950*
*(Text page 74)*

*The old school at the main road, Cardross (Text page 75)*

*A Cardross School class about 1922 (Text page 77)*

48

*Primary I Class, Cardross School about 1930 (Text page 77)*

49

*Andersons the Newsagents Shop about 1936 (Text page 78)*

*The centre of Cardross about 1932 (Text page 78)*

50

*The old Smithy house at the end of Smithy Road (Text page 79)*

51

57

52

*Cardross around Beatrice Villa (Muirholm) at the beginning of this century*
*(Text page 79)*

53

58    *The main road, Cardross, from Woodneuk, looking west to Hope Terrace, about*
*1930 (Text page 80)*

*The main road, Cardross, looking east from Hope Terrace around the turn of the century (Text page 80)*

54

NORTH END, CARDROSS.

*The Geilston area with Kirkton Road Cottage about 1906 (Text page 80)*

55

59

56

*"Rockwell"* (*Geilston Hall Cottage*) *today* (*Text page 80*)

57

*The Geilston Hall about 1930* (*Text page 80*)

60

58

*East door, Geilston Hall, showing commemorative plaque (Text page 80)*

59

*Kilmahew Mill ca 1900 (Text page 81)*

61

60

*Kilmahew Chapel after restoration* (*Text pages 81-82*)

61

62

*Interior of Kilmahew Chapel after restoration* (*Text pages 81-82*)

*Kilmahew Mansion House about 1900 (Text pages 82-83)*

*Kilmahew from the Swan Pond about 1900*

64

*Murrays Farm in the early years of this century (Text page 84)*

*Geilston House today (Text page 85)*

66

*John Graham, chauffeur, with David Murray's car at Moore Park about 1914*
*(Text page 86)*

67

*Ardardan House between the wars (Text page 86)*

68

*Drumhead House today (Text page 86)*
*Photo: Mitchell & Averell, Dumbarton*

67

69

*Lyleston House today* (*Text page 86*)

70

*Keppoch House today* (*Text pages 86-87*)

71

*Harvesting at Lyleston Farm at the beginning of this century* (*Text page 88*)

69

72

*Low Auchensail Farm at the beginning of this century* (*Text page 88*)

four semi-detached houses (facing the station), in the last of which the young A.J. Cronin once stayed.

On the right after the church, and beyond Church Avenue, stands the Victorian semi-detached house known as "Mayfield", and next to it an Edwardian house. A lane then leads to modern houses, and next is the Victorian house now called "Dana Cottage", once the home of Hutchison the coal merchant whose yard was adjacent. At the beginning of this century the house incorporated the Post Office. New housing developments are taking place in this area. A railway yard concludes this side of the road. In late Victorian times there was a nursery to the west of "Dana Cottage".

Our photograph (ill. 37) shows Station Road about 1905 looking north from "Dana Cottage", then the Post Office run by J. West. It is worth reflecting at this point that only 120 years ago the only building on Station Road was the small cottage mentioned at the beginning of this section.

## THE RAILWAY

We have now reached the railway station. The railway, it should be remembered, was largely responsible for the development of Cardross village in Victorian times. As early as 1853 a public meeting was held to discuss the proposed Glasgow, Dumbarton & Helensburgh Railway Company. The related Parliamentary Bill received the Royal assent in 1855, and the contractors, John Barr & Co. of Ardrossan, began work on the Dalreoch tunnel right away. The ground was broken as far as Cardross by early 1856 and by July of that year the operating line had been carried, with only a few breaks, as far as the village. Work from the Helensburgh end started early in 1857 and progress from that date was rapid.

On the 15th of January 1858, before the official opening date, some guests present at the Cardross ploughing match and dinner were conveyed by steam train from Cardross to Dumbarton through the Dalreoch tunnel, the first passenger journey for people not connected with the construction of the line. Goods traffic commenced on the 25th of May that year and soon after, the extension of telegraphic wires along the line was completed.

Finally, only 2¾ years after operations had begun, the line was officially opened for passenger traffic on Monday the 31st May 1858. There was some early disquiet in the village about timetabling, but soon the line was affording general satisfaction. The line was doubled by May 1883. A railway bridge at the station was not built until 1884, and before that date there were some nasty accidents on the crossing at the end of Station Road.

As well as encouraging increased feuing in Cardross together with the development of housing, the railway also brought a number of new occupations to the area. There was a stationmaster, a clerk, a porter, and there were signalmen at Cardross Station and at Ardmore; several railway surfacemen and labourers also settled in and around the village, some families residing in the area for a considerable period. For example, Peter Keough, who resided in a little cottage at the end of the Murrays road, retired in 1931 after 42 years' service with the North British Railway Company and the L.N.E.R. Stationmaster Thomas Taylor retired in 1932 after 26 years' service at Cardross and was succeeded by James Barnes. Both will be remembered by older residents.

Our first railway photograph (ill. 38) shows the station building around 1913. This is the building which, with some alterations, still stands, and it is the original 1858 structure. The waiting-room on the south platform stood until 1979. Some of the station staff have lined up for the photograph. A group of Cardross railway employees can be seen in the next photograph (ill. 39) of about the same date. The names, as far as I can ascertain, are: back row (left to right), Kelly, W. Oswald, McLeod (?), Matthew Hutchison, Thomson; front row (left to right), Edward Camlin, Thomas Taylor (stationmaster), J. Logan.

Finally, (ill. 40) some employees can be seen at Cardross signal box on 1st of June 1923. The young man second from the right is Samuel Davis, clerk.

The line, which had passed to the North British and then to the L.N.E.R., became part of the nationalised network of British Railways in 1948. Electrification came in 1960 and the designation "British Rail" in 1964. West Highland diesel trains often thunder past the village, but for them Cardross station is not a stopping point.

★ ★ ★ ★ ★ ★ ★ ★ ★ ★

If we cross the railway bridge at Cardross station we reach the shore. The piece of ground immediately to the south and south-east of the station, though it had been available at times for recreational purposes for many decades, was finally gifted as a recreation ground by Major Burns of Kilmahew in 1919 at the time when he sold the estate. It was known for a time as the Burns Park. The area has been a favourite resort for summer day-trippers from Glasgow and elsewhere for many years.

A path leads eastwards from the park area to join the stone bridge over the railway at the end of Ferry Road. At the end of Peel Street an iron railway footbridge gives access to the shore. The original bridge here, erected in 1885, was the result of a right-of-way dispute which flared up at the beginning of that year. A railway barricade had been erected by the Company, blocking a crossing, and on various occasions villagers (sometimes assisted by experienced Vale of Leven men) arrived in force to pull it down. The barricade was re-erected and strengthened and on one occasion the villagers met a defending force of 27 railway officers and some County Constabulary men. A lively exchange of views followed. Finally in February a meeting was held in the Free Church schoolroom and a committee elected to correspond with the railway company. As a result a footbridge was erected and the existing crossing kept for cart traffic.

On the stony beach, nearly opposite this point, can be seen a marker shaped like an Iona cross. This marks the limit of the jurisdiction of the Clyde Navigation Trust over the river. Its opposite number stands near Newark Castle.

A path also leads westwards from the shore park past some neat cottages one or two of which, around the middle of last century, housed some workers connected with a neighbouring brick and tile works. The sawmills occupy the latter site today. The path continues towards the old Murrays farm buildings, and beyond, and is a favourite with Sunday walkers and (nowadays) people on horseback. Our photograph (ill. 41) shows Cardross shore from a point just west of the footbridge over the Geilston Burn. The station can be seen towards the right.

While discussing Cardross shore mention must be made of the one-time Whelk (or "Wulk") Fair, an ancient institution the origins of which are lost in "antiquity". There seems to have been a connection (at least in Victorian times) with the annual Bonhill sacramental Fast Day at the end of April or beginning of May, when all the print and dye works in the Vale of Leven were closed, and many Vale folk came over the hill. Some went down to the shore to gather shell fish. Gathering the whelks had, however, been a local occupation of Cardross women for a long time before that, some having wandered out at low tide as far as the sandbanks. In 1882 it was reported that "some of the toilers of the sea succeeded in turning an honest penny". In that year many Vale children held picnic parties. At the 1889 Whelk Fair nearly all the riveters, blacksmiths, and fitters in the Dumbarton shipyards were made idle because the rivet boys and apprentices decided to take a holiday and attend the Fair.

The shell fish gathering aspect of the Fair had, during last century, been supplemented by the presence of stalls and booths. There was dancing and there was music; amusements included donkey rides, swing boats, games of skill and sleight of hand. In 1916, though the event was declining, there was an air-gun shooting range and a roulette wheel. In 1925, however, there were no stalls and the shore was deserted. Nevertheless, the custom of enjoying picnic parties on the shore on the day of the Fair persisted, weather permitting, into the 1930s, and attempts were even made to re-establish the old custom.

The brick and tile works already mentioned were set up in the late 1850s as a result of various factors including the suitability of local clay, the nearby railway siding, and the numerous building projects. Near the end of the Murrays road there was, at the same period, another tile works possessed for a time by Alexander McIntyre. Each works had a large crane and Cardross shore in these days must have had a busier and almost industrial appearance.

Camping of various kinds and in varying degrees of semi-permanence was long a feature of Cardross shore. More permanent dwellings have, well into this century, given rise to disputes as to rights there and ownership of the shore. In the 1920s summer camping was considerable. A journalist with the "Helensburgh and Gareloch Times" wrote in July 1922:

"The community starts at the west end of Cardross, where about thirty tents are pitched adjacent to the Burns Park. Opposite Cardross Station animated scenes are witnessed daily between the campers and the day trippers; dozens of fires being kept going for cooking purposes. Here also are numerous stalls for providing refreshments in the form of ice-cream, aerated waters, confections, etc., all doing good business. Crossing Geilston Burn, the tents are more congested for about a mile along, all of various shapes and sizes, good, bad and indifferent, many neither wind nor water-tight, composed principally of sacking, ground sheets, and any other like material. A favourite form is large tarpaulin, which provide a roomy, comfortable bivouac. The feature among this lot of temporary dwellings is the artistic taste developed, many of the occupants vieing with one another in the decoration of ground surrounding their tents. The work is done in sand, shells, and white pebbles, the name of the tent, or the cognomen by which the occupants choose to be known, being neatly figured out and bordered."

Many and varied have been the activities connected with Cardross shore. I am told that for a while between the wars there was even dog-racing of an unofficial kind in the field immediately west of the Geilston Burn. Duck shooting was a favourite occupation at the shore for amateur and professional sportsmen particularly in the first half of last century. The men often went out in small sailing craft. The advent of busy steam navigation on the Clyde, however, resulted in the virtual desertion of the area by many species of shore birds. In more recent times the area has again become an interesting haunt for birdwatchers.

Where the aforementioned brick and tile works once stood can today be seen the Cardross Sawmills. Sawmilling was for many a long year connected with the McIntyre family in Cardross, the business having been started in 1827 by Archibald McIntyre (d.1847) who came from Glenorchy in Argyllshire in the early part of last century to settle at Geilston. The house "Woodneuk" at Geilston was built and occupied by the family, and the business of sawmilling soon established. When Archibald McIntyre died the business was run for a while by his widow and by a relative of her husband until her eldest son John was of age to take over. He gave his name to the firm of John McIntyre & Son, a firm which soon attracted an impressive list of customers including all the major Clydeside shipbuilders. The amount of work undertaken, including sawmilling, joinery and carpentry, was extraordinary, ranging from humble fence and house repairs locally, to the supply of large timbers for the hulks of wooden vessels and more finished timbers for the woodwork in iron ships.

Some timber came from local woods but much was brought from Argyll. In addition, the McIntyres worked Murrays Farm for many years and were involved in traditional grain milling for a while. The old Kilmahew grain mill (in Geilston Glen) had been acquired and the sawmill business was mainly carried on there until the premises were destroyed by fire in 1912. (This will be discussed when we reach Geilston).

Soon after this calamity the firm moved into the premises at the shore. We have two photographs of the workforce about 1920. In the first (ill. 42) some of the men have been identified. At the far left is Jack McIntyre of the family firm. Next to him is James Davis the engineman, and third from the right, Jimmy McIntyre the sawyer. Second from the right stands the foreman Jock Adamson, and at the far right, the then head of the firm, Archibald McIntyre. Perhaps more interesting is the second group photograph (ill. 43) in which the workmen display their tools of the trade. At the far left stands Jimmy McIntyre, chief sawyer (later to become foreman), and beside him Jock Adamson, foreman, stands with the rule book in his hands! James Davis, engineman, is second from the right with his oil can.

Fire is always a hazard for sawmills and in June 1927 a bad conflagration destroyed the buildings. It took the Helensburgh and Dumbarton Fire Brigades two hours to subdue the flames. New buildings were, however, erected and our next photograph (ill. 44) gives a good idea of the extent of the business about 1947.

The decline of shipbuilding on the Clyde was a severe blow to the firm which had been carried on by a succession of Archibalds and Johns for five generations. Archibald McIntyre of "Glenlee" Cardross still runs a timber merchant's business from his home; but from 1974 the sawmills at the shore have been in the possession of Mr. Alfred Riding — and seem to be flourishing. The smell of wood and sawdust is still a pleasant feature of a walk along the shore in the vicinity of the Geilston Burn.

If we walk back along Station Road we reach Church Avenue on the left. This attractive road contains a variety of houses of different styles and periods. The east end of the avenue dates from 1872 when John William Burns of Kilmahew made the fields available for feuing purposes, but the west end of the road was not completed until the end of last century when the golf course there was discontinued. The line of houses on the north side is now complete as far as Reay Avenue, and includes one or two very recent houses which tastefully blend in with the red sandstone of earlier buildings. On the south side much of the ground has been laid out for recreational purposes.

On this side we see first the green of Cardross Bowling Club. There was a club in Cardross in the early 1930s, but a new club was formed in 1939 and the premises here formally inaugurated on Saturday the 1st of June, 1940. Lady Denny, wife of Sir Maurice Denny, threw the first bowl. Mr. Robert Boyd was the first President, and Mr. Robert Nicholson the first club champion, winning the Kilmahew Cup in 1940.

Next we come to the grounds of the Cardross Tennis Club which has been flourishing since the early 1970s. There are three courts, the last (furthest west) having been opened as recently as 1979.

The grounds on which the bowling green and tennis courts are laid out, together with the sports field to the south, are Cardross Trust property, this dating from a gift of land there in 1937 by Dr. Johnstone Smith of Ardardan. Eunice Murray of Moore Park had tried unsuccessfully in 1933 to get a similar recreational project started in the fields adjacent to Cardross Park mansion house.

To the south of the bowling green and the tennis courts can be seen the football ground which is entered from Station Road. Football has been played in Cardross for many years. In 1913 a match was played between Hermitage School and Cardross, resulting in a 2-2 draw. The Cardross team on that occasion was: Crane, McFarlane, and J. McNaughton; R. McNaughton and E. Kelly; J. Adie, Davie, L. McArthur, A. McArthur, and A. Adie. A boys' team existed in 1922 when the following are recorded as having played against St. Joseph's, Helensburgh: Graham, McGregor & Gemmell; Emmerson, McPherson and R. Thomson; McCondachie, McFarlane, Purdie, W. Thomson, and Bulloch. A team called Cardross Accies existed in 1925 and one called Cardross Villa in 1930.

The better-known Cardross Rovers Football Club was inaugurated in 1938 with James Graham as President. The team reached some prominence in local amateur circles by winning the Lochside League Cup in 1950. The winning team is pictured (ill. 45): back row, left to right, Alex Walker (manager, now resides at "Glenavondale", Church Avenue), Alan Phillips, Edward Ashman, Jim McPherson, Jimmy Kirkwood, Jim Retson, Mat Ashman, Mat Emmerson (trainer); second row, left to right, Drew Purdie, William ("Sony") Thomson, Bobby Phillips, Jim McIntyre, Archie Mills; front row, left to right, the ball boys Jimmy McPherson, Stewart Walker, and Willie McPherson. In the 1950s the club played an annual match against

Nettleham in Lincolnshire on an alternate home and away basis. Some present day Cardross residents will remember when the Lincoln boys were "in town". In more recent times the Cardross Rock Football Club has been using the pitch.

Let us return to the main highway at the top of Station Road, and proceed westwards. On the left stands the tenement called "Villafield". Before it was erected in about 1890 a house of the same name stood here. The tenement did not please a Helensburgh journalist who wrote in May 1890:

> "The village of Cardross, which promised for long to be an exception to the almost universal blunder of placing huge (sic) tenements — a real curse of Scotland — in country places, has fallen from its high estate, and now has its common three-storey tenements."

The building is, however, not unattractive. A number of shops have occupied the ground floor over the years. On the corner the one-time grocer's shop is now Cardross Branch Library. As a grocer's shop it had at one time been occupied by the McIntyre family. Duncan McIntyre (d.1897), a brother of John McIntyre of the Cardross Sawmills, was grocer, postmaster, and provision merchant in Cardross until his death. His widow and his son John carried on the business for many years. Even when Gladwell occupied the shop in the 1960s the name "McIntyre" was still displayed. Mr. Brownlie was the last grocer there until the late 1970s. The next shop was once the Post Office run by Bob Buchanan, tailor, between the wars. Anderson the newsagent ran the Post Office across the road for part of the war period, and Kate and Jean McGlashan afterwards took over in the old "Villafield" shop. Some people will remember Dalling the baker's shop which was the next along. From about 1887 until 1937 this was McKinstry the baker's shop. There was a cobbler's business in the last shop until the 1950s.

After "Villafield" we come to the modern Post Office built on the site of Jimmy Lyle the plumber's premises. Bobby Brander occupied this Post Office until very recently. The old 18th century house called "Broomfield" follows. A well-known Cardross centenarian Mrs. Isabella ("Granny") Lawrance (born 1860) lived here latterly. Then comes an old garage building which was long occupied by George Fraser and family. There were petrol pumps in front until the 1960s. The next building, "Laigh Barrs" (built on one of the lower fields of the one-time Barrs Farm), probably dates from the 18th century. "Broomfield" and "Laigh Barrs" may both have been built when the Edmonstones occupied Cardross Park. The aforementioned George Fraser had a grocer's shop here in the first half of this century, followed by Jimmy Gibson. The County Branch Library was here before the District Library Service moved it to "Villafield". Curtains are now sold in this shop, prior to which it was used for a short time as a coffee house.

## CARDROSS SCHOOL

We have now reached the site of the old Cardross School (ill. 46) which was demolished only this year. At this point we might pause to reflect briefly on the history of schooling in the area.

What educational provision there was at the Kirkton at Levengrove until 1644 is not known. However, in 1632, Robert Napier of Kilmahew offered the then already disused Chapel of Kilmahew as a school for the children of the area. He was to pay for the upkeep of the school twice a year, and pay the schoolmaster who was also given some adjacent land for grazing a cow. A dwelling house was built nearby before the completion of which the new dominie stayed at Kilmahew Castle with the laird and conducted family prayers. A barn was converted for his house, and it is interesting to note that Kirkton Cottage, for many years and until very recently the head teacher's house, is built on the very same site.

The Kilmahew Chapel building was used only until the early 19th century when a new school was built where we are now standing at the south of the main road. However, this move did not alter the educational ideals and pre-suppositions which had dominated the educational world in Scotland for centuries. The syllabus and teaching side of school life was controlled by (though not performed by) the parish church, while the financial side (just as it had been in the days of Robert Napier of Kilmahew), upkeep of property, and so on, was the preserve of the local heritors. It was part of the minister's duties to visit the school and catechise the pupils, and he was expected to keep a close eye on the orthodoxy of the schoolmaster's religious beliefs. The dominie could easily be dismissed, and if this was his misfortune, his chances of similar employment elsewhere were slim. Even after the Education Act of 1803 which brought in a number of new measures, the appointment of a teacher had to be approved by the local Presbytery, and the appointee had to sign the Confession of Faith and the formula of the established Church of Scotland. It was because of this test that the Free Church of Scotland set up schools of their own shortly after the Disruption of 1843. The theological test was later removed, and when the Education Act of 1872 made non-denominational educational provision compulsory on a parish basis, the pressing need for church-based schools was removed.

By the 1850s Cardross Parish School was still being examined annually by a committee of the Presbytery of Dumbarton. In 1862 there were nearly 100 pupils who were praised by the committee for their proficiency in grammar and in writing on slates to dictation. At that time Robert Buchanan (of whom more hereafter) was headmaster and a Miss Howat was the certified teacher of the first class. She also instructed the girls in sewing and knitting in the afternoons. At the end of these inspections it was customary for the children to receive an ample quantity of buns as a treat, these being supplied by one of the local ladies. However as early as this, the secular involvement with parish education was well under way. There were various sub-inspectors of schools for Scotland who visited periodically.

The big change in the parish generally and in Cardross village in particular came with the Education (Scotland) Act of 1872. In March 1873 there was a meeting of the qualified heritors and the Minister to fix a time and place for the election of a Cardross School Board, as required under the Act. There were public meetings arranged to explain the provisions of the Act to the villagers of Cardross and Renton. The following was the result of the first School Board election held on the 19th April 1873:

Successful candidates —

| | |
|---|---|
| J.W. Burns, Kilmahew | 655 |
| Rev. Alex. Cameron, Gaelic Free Church, Renton | 527 |
| Rev. William Dunn, Cardross | 499 |
| Rev. W.M. Dempster, Free Church, Renton | 396 |
| J.M. Martin, Auchenfroe | 382 |
| Rev. Michael Fox, R.C. Clergyman, Alexandria | 336 |
| David Paul, engineer, Renton | 297 |

After the result was declared, J.W. Burns was borne shoulder-high to his carriage waiting outside Renton School.

In 1874 the school building was improved and extended, the architect being John McLeod of Dumbarton. The official opening took place on the 7th of December that year. There were now five classrooms and a large playground and the school could accommodate 210 pupils instead of the previous 110. The building was further extended at the end of the century (ill. 46). To commemorate the coronation of George V, a flagstaff was erected in 1911. It is interesting to note that around that time the headmaster's salary was £200 per annum — not bad for those days.

Evening continuation classes had by this time been formed. The compulsory nature of school attendance had by then taken a grip of the minds of children and parents, and when in 1912 eight schoolboys were reported to have been employed by local landowners as pheasant beaters during a shooting session (for which they had received 3/- plus luncheon), the headmaster, Mr. Pollock, complained, and the gentlemen were written to in no uncertain terms.

Eunice Murray of Moore Park, who was active on the Education Committee for many years, was in 1914 advocating more practical and domestic classes particularly for girls to prepare them for "the world". In the early 1920s school activities were further increased when headmaster R.P. Kinloch organised a choir in connection with the evening continuation classes, and many concerts were held.

Electricity was installed in 1929. Pupils who went on to secondary education in the earlier part of the century often attended Dumbarton Academy, St. Patrick's High School, Dumbarton, or Notre Dame School for Girls, Dumbarton. Nowadays Hermitage Academy, Helensburgh, takes most of the pupils from the Cardross area.

The headmasters of the old school on the main road were:

1. Robert Buchanan c1846-1889. He was born in the West Bridgend district of the parish and became a much loved and respected character in the village. He was also Session Clerk of Cardross Parish Church for 40 years and was for many years Registrar of Births, Deaths, and Marriages. When he retired he moved from the schoolhouse at Kirkton to Church Avenue where he died in 1893.

2. John Smith 1889-1912.

3. James MacDougall Pollock 1912-1914.

4. Robert Parlane Kinloch 1914-1929.

5. John Donald 1929-1942.

6. Ian McKinnon 1948-   (also first headmaster of the new school).

In 1957 part of a new school at the top of Kirkton Road was opened and occupied by the primary department. The building was completed and officially opened on the 6th of March 1959 by ex-Provost John M. Jack of Helensburgh. This had accommodation for 240 pupils with 8 classrooms, one general purposes room, an assembly hall, a kitchen and a dining hall, plus several stores. Work began immediately on preparing a large playing field to the north. The old school did not, however, lie empty, but was used in recent years as a skill centre.

Before leaving this subject let us look at two old photographs (ills. 47 & 48) of Cardross school classes. The first, taken probably in 1922, contains some individuals whom I have been able to identify: back row, left to right, Alex Walker; Alastair Archibald; Lennie McGregor; —— Emmerson; Gavin Davis; —?—; second row, left to right, Charlie McGregor; ?; Margaret Ramsay; —— Grieve?; —?—; Dan Purdie; third row, left to right, Jenny McKinstry; Ena Hayes; Ellen Moir; Margaret McInnes; Marion Emmerson; —?—; Peggy Miller; front row, left to right, Willie Cole; Andrew Potter; —?—; Alistair Johnston.

Our second group photo, taken probably in 1930, shows a primary one class. Those identified are: back row, left to right: Donald McLeod, Ian McIndoe, Willie McGrath, Willie Adie, James Adie, George McFarlane, Tom McGall, Arthur Bell, Donald McNicol; second row, left to right, Peggy Meikle, Agnes Clark, Mabel Archibald, Cathie McPherson, ?, ?, Edith Ashman, Edith McPherson, Greta Lyle, Betty Crane; front row, left to right, Alan Paisley, Peter McFarlane, David McIndoe, Duncan McPherson, ?, ?, Bertie Dunbar, ?, Hugh McPherson, Robert McBride.

★ ★ ★ ★ ★ ★ ★ ★ ★ ★ ★ ★ ★ ★ ★

Across the road from the already-mentioned garage building now stands a modern filling station originally established by the Frasers, and under its present ownership providing an excellent service to the motorist.

77

Behind this is a small and pleasant council housing estate built in the 1960s in part of the grounds of Cardross Park. On this side of the main road, nearly opposite the site of the old school, once stood Cardross Park West Lodge pictured (ill. 29) about 1938. Next on this side of the road still stands a purpose-built shop which dates from the beginning of the 1920s having been erected for Bob McMeekin. A family called Donnan succeeded. In our photograph (ill. 49) taken about 1936, Mrs Anderson, one of the early occupants of the shop, can be seen in the middle with Nancy Lyle on the left and Mrs Anderson's daughter on the right. The shop was in these days a newsagent's and drapery store. On the right of the photo can be seen the first public telephone kiosk in Cardross, placed there in 1934 in response to considerable demand.

If we stand near the side of the road a little further on and look back, we will be in the position for the photographer of our next photograph (ill. 50) taken about 1932. From the left we see the above-mentioned shop and Cardross Park West Lodge; from the right, the school (with the children crowding on to the road), "Laigh Barrs" (in front of which stands another group of interested spectators), "Broomfield", and "Villafield". The quality of this print is not very good but it does give an idea of how much more peaceful and rural the centre of the village appeared in these years.

Shortly after the shop Muirend Road goes off to the right leading to numerous private housing developments which were begun in the 1960s and which by now are quite extensive having spread some distance uphill. Indeed most people in Cardross now live either in the Bainfield estate or in this area together with the adjacent council housing estate immediately to the west. Back at the main road, some attractive bungalows built in the early 1930s occupy the area between Muirend Road and Barrs Road.

Returning to the site of the old school, the next on the left is a two-storey red sandstone building with houses above and shops below. The butcher's shop of Hugh Mills Davie has been there for a considerable number of years. The previous butcher was a Mr. Wilson, and before that, Dougie Lamont. The next shop was Gibson's the licensed grocer for many years, having previously been the premises of the Royal Bank and before that, the Commercial Bank. Next is a modern Bank of Scotland building followed by two late Victorian villas containing together four semi-detached houses, and then comes the bungalow called "Luzon". Between this house and the Police Station lies one half acre of ground gifted in 1937 by Dr. Johnstone Smith of Ardardan as an open space to be landscaped. This is today a very pretty spot where it is worth while pausing for a rest.

At the Police Station let us turn left down Reay Avenue. This short street was laid out in Edwardian times and contains attractive houses. A gate at the south end leads into a field adjacent to the football ground. This field was once part of the original Cardross Golf Course, but is now used for grazing purposes. Near the gate stands the scout hall. At the other end of the avenue there is the police house and station. Cardross did not have a resident policeman until 1853. As a result of complaints to the Commissioners of Supply for the county by Colin Campbell of Colgrain, A.B. Yuille of Darleith, and others, chiefly concerning raids on the area by tinkers, a policeman was settled in the village. Duncan McColl was the first officer. Sergeant Clark of "Glenview", Cardross, served from 1898 to 1922 in the village and will be well remembered by some older residents. Mention should be made of Dougie Taylor and of Donald Macaulay in more recent times who served with friendly distinction. The police house we see here was erected for the County Council in 1924, with Alex. McPhail the first officer there.

After the small British Legion Hall at the main road, Smithy Road goes off to the left. This little road was built up in Victorian times by the Burns family of Kilmahew who owned the land. There are some attractive cottages including "Rose Cottage" which has for many years been occupied by the Camlin family the first member of which to come to Cardross, William Camlin, established a builder's business in the village. He was much involved in the construction of Church Avenue over 100 years ago. The smithy once stood at the foot of the road. As has been mentioned the smithy was before this at the east end of the village. William Stirton, a

Perthshire man, was the first village blacksmith at the new site having come from Glasgow in 1875. The smithy house was built in 1883 (ill. 51). Jock Heggison was the last blacksmith and farrier here. Alexander McRae once had a joiner's business in this vicinity well into the present century, and more recently Ritchie the housebuilder established his offices here. Luxury flats have very recently been built on the site with the name "Smithy Court".

Back at the main road we continue westwards. On the left the cottage which we reach first is probably the oldest building in this stretch — probably early 19th century. The next two buildings were erected in the late 1850s for James Burns of Kilmahew and the whole area here is known as Burnsland. In the first there were, between the wars, two shops, one of them Johnston's which sold groceries and confections. The Co-operative Society took over in the 1930s. After the next 1850s building stands a 2-storey red sandstone tenement with houses and a general store. Another red sandstone building follows and at one time there was yet another beyond called "The Balcony" (because there was such a feature at the second storey) which stood till some twenty years ago. The last three buildings were a further housing development for which the Burns family was responsible, and were constructed about 1872. Two modern semi-detached houses now stand on the site of "The Balcony". Finally a very recent bungalow aptly called "Burnsland" completes the row of houses on this side before the Geilston Burn. It is worth recording here that at one time the houses at Burnsland were very crowded indeed with families of artisans and labouring folk. In 1891, for example, the buildings were divided into 18 houses then occupied by 17 families — 61 people in all.

If we return to the beginning of Barrs Road (which was blocked off some ten years ago) we can follow the houses on the right of the main road. The Muirholm Hotel comes first. It was built over 100 years ago as a wedding gift to a lady called Beatrice Campbell, and was known initially as "Beatrice Villa". "Beatrice Villa" eventually became "Muirholm" and was converted for use as a hotel in the mid 1960s after having for a while provided Bed and Breakfast accommodation.

The houses next to the Muirholm Hotel were erected on the site of Edwardian semi-detached villas destroyed in the Cardross blitz. Our photograph (ill. 52), taken early in the first decade of the present century shows "Beatrice Villa" on the right, part of Smithy Road on the left, and Burnsland in the middle. There were plots for a while in the bit of ground at the left beside Smithy Road.

Further along the main road on the right stand the council houses known as Barrs Crescent, built in 1925 — the first council houses in the village. These were followed by the council houses near the foot of Barrs Road and by the first two buildings round the corner in Barrs Terrace erected at the end of the 1920s. Soon after the south side of Barrs Terrace was completed and after the war a large area between Barrs Road, Kirkton Road, and Darleith Road was built up on fields once belonging to the former Barrs Farm. Barrs Road was at one time the farm access lane.

Back at Geilston Bridge we are in the area known as Geilston from time immemorial. The name means the "tun" or farm enclosure of the "ghillies" or farm servants, and there were most probably common grazing grounds in this area. It is a mere verbal coincidence that for so many years last century a family called Geils owned the estate — though their presence may well have been responsible for fixing the spelling of the name "Geilston".

The first house on the left at the foot of the brae is "Woodneuk", probably about 150 years old. Here at one time lived the McIntyres who had the already-mentioned saw-milling business. Their joinery and carpentry shops were to the east of the house with the stables at the west. Next comes a modern bungalow. In this area there used to be two small cottages; the second, occupied by a Miss McIntyre, contained a sweetie shop known as "Peggy Buntin's" after the maiden name of a forebear who lived there throughout much of the Victorian period. These cottages together with some other property in the area appear to have been owned by one, Donald Keith, around the middle of last century, and were sometimes referred to as "Keith's Cottages" or "Keith's Land".

The four semi-detached houses which now follow stand on the site of an ancient tenement known as "Hope Terrace" (ills. 53 & 54) which was destroyed in the air raids of 1941. At the end of last century the houses were sometimes referred to as "Jackson's Land" after the then proprietor. The property was advertised for sale in 1935 when it consisted of two houses of two rooms and kitchen and four houses of one room and kitchen. The asking price was £400.

Finally on the left stands the old cottage called "Glengate" (after the nearby Geilston Glen). An adjacent path leads through a small wood to connect with the Murrays Road. This can provide a pleasant stroll in summer provided there has not been much rain — otherwise the track will be found churned up by horse traffic!

Let us now cross over and return to the bottom of Darleith Road. Here we can see a small pleasantly-landscaped area. A group of cottages built in the early 19th century, or maybe before, stood here until a few years after the last war. Right at the corner, at an angle, stood Kirkton Road Cottage. (At one time Darleith Road was called Kirkton Road, hence the name). It is the main feature of one of our photographs (ill. 55) taken in the very early years of this century. In pre-railway days this was known as the old Geilston Change House. The stage coach running between Dumbarton and Helensburgh stopped here so that the travellers and horses alike could have their thirst quenched. Attached to both ends of the main cottage were one-storey houses which at one time were occupied mainly by agricultural labourers and their families. Writing in 1901, Dr. McLachlan mentioned the occupant, twenty years before that, of the but and ben furthest up the Darleith Road. This was old Rob Ewing, "a quaint, canty carle, in his way, a bachelor, fond of a joke, a dram, and a snuff." He seems to have been a jack of all trades, turning his hand at blacksmithing, shoe mending, horticulture, and (apparently for amusement), stocking knitting!

As has been mentioned before the main part of Kirkton Road Cottage was used as a salvage depot during the last war. Some may remember the earlier connection of the Cole and Leckie families with this house.

Another small cottage stood between Kirkton Road Cottage and the Geilston Burn and another just beyond the stream. The next cottage in this small area actually still stands and is named "Rockwell" (ill. 56). As was the case with all these old properties (and with those across the road), this house has been referred to by various names and descriptions over the years, but it was perhaps best known as Geilston Hall Cottage. Next we see the premises of a joinery run for many years by the firm of Boyd and Wilson. These stand right beside the Geilston Hall.

We have had occasion to mention the Geilston Hall (ills. 57 & 58) in this history many times. The amount of concerts, meetings, assemblies, etc., etc., which have taken place here over the years is truly enormous. The first building on this site was a spacious wooden Drill Hall built by Major Geils of Geilston in 1863-4 to house the new Company of Cardross Volunteers. While this remained the main purpose of the building, many other events took place there in the Victorian era — meetings of temperance societies, religious groups, Good Templars, etc. A series of winter lectures ran for many years, covering all sorts of subjects. A library was kept in the hall for use by the villagers. This first hall, which was owned by Mrs Geils of Geilston House, was destroyed by fire on the 7th of March 1889.

Only two months later preparations were being made for the erection of a new hall as a necessary amenity for the village, and on the 30th of July that year a commemorative stone was laid. The new halls, designed by Messrs Honeyman and Keppie, were already well advanced. The stone was laid by Miss Catherine Geils and there was a short service of praise and prayer. The building was in use by the following year and the various activities which had taken place in the old wooden Drill Hall were resumed. The new building was still referred to as the Drill Hall for quite some time. It is unnecessary to go into any detail about the many events which have taken place there under the auspices of the Geilston Hall Trust except perhaps to record the interesting fact that the young Stanley Baxter (then aged 9) performed impersonations of Harry Lauder and Dave Willis at a Girls Association Concert on 12th December 1935.

Let us return to the foot of Geilston brae and walk up Darleith Road. This road was sometimes called Kirkton Road since it led to the chapel of Kirkton of Kilmahew and to Kirkton Farm. There is now a different Kirkton Road in the council housing scheme nearby. Sometimes Darleith Road was referred to as the Mill Road after Kilmahew Mill which once stood in Geilston Glen down the steep embankment to the left and in among the trees. The old mill (ill. 59) was once the grain or corn mill (and also, for a time, lintmill) for the farms on the estate of Kilmahew, and was occupied by a family called Glen who were in possession for much of the eighteenth century, and during the nineteenth century until 1860. For example, old Walter Glen who had worked there all his working life, died in 1852 aged 78. The McIntyres of the Cardross Sawmills seem to have had premises adjacent to the old building earlier than that and eventually took over the grain mill too after Robert Fulton's term there between 1860 and 1871. In the photograph, the main building shown was the old corn mill, while the wooden building lower down on the left was the sawmill as such. On the evening of 9th February 1912 a disastrous fire struck, having originated in the boiler house. The wooden sawmill was totally consumed and the old stone building was completely gutted. The shell remained for a number of years. The Helensburgh and Dumbarton Fire Brigades were able to do little. Soon after, the sawmilling business was removed to Cardross Shore.

I am told that Geilston Glen was, with its well, trysting tree, and winding paths, the haunt of many courting couples and sweethearts — a romantic spot indeed.

Walking past the council houses on the right we continue along the road until we reach the old cottage of "Westlade", recently extended. It was once occupied by sawmill employees and their families. Further up on the right is the large late-Victorian villa "Edindonach", built for Duncan McRae McIntyre, grocer, and down on the left a house on the site of the one-time Glen Nursery. Behind this house can be seen the dam which served Kilmahew Mill.

Moving on into the countryside, past some bungalows on the right, we eventually reach the area known as Kirkton and see the beautiful little white-washed church called Kirkton Chapel or Kilmahew Chapel. Near the church stands Kirkton Cottage which was for many years the schoolmaster's house. Just before the church a road goes off to the right to Kirkton Farm, and opposite the chapel a road branches off to the left to Drumhead House.

Kilmahew or Kirkton Chapel (ill. 60) has had an interesting history of which there is only space here to give a brief account. The site was, by the 5th century A.D. probably remembered as that of an old pagan sanctuary, and it is likely that a little unpretentious church was soon after established here by followers of St. Mochta (or by St. Mochta himself), a disciple of St. Patrick. "Mochta" was corrupted to "Mahew" and the church (Cill) became known as Kilmahew, the name eventually applying to the surrounding lands which took on the identity of an estate in feudal times. The chapel, or some later version of it, must have been in a state of disrepair by the 15th century for Duncan Napier of Kilmahew had it rebuilt then, and it was consecrated on the 10th of May 1467 by the Bishop of Argyll.

After the Reformation it became a Protestant chapel-of-ease (hence "chapel") with a Reader in charge on behalf of the Minister of Rosneath, towards the end of the 16th century; for it is to be remembered that the church was within Rosneath Parish at that time. When, in the middle of the following century, the parish of Cardross was extended to include all this area and a parish church was built on the site at the east end of Cardross village, the old chapel was converted for use as a parochial school. The surrounding burial ground, however, remained in use for some years. After about 1846 the chapel ceased to be used for school purposes and fell into ruin.

In 1948 the Archdiocese of Glasgow acquired the land on which the ruin stood and soon after planned to have the old place of worship restored. Work began in 1953 under the direction of Ian G. Lindsay & Partners, Edinburgh. The style of the medieval church was followed externally and in many internal particulars; a small vestry was added to the north side and the nave extended at the west end, the gable there being surmounted by a small belfry. In 1955 an ancient standing stone was, by chance, dug up, on which was inscribed the cross of St. Mahew. This interesting relic is preserved in the vestibule of the reconstructed church.

On Sunday the 22nd of May 1955 the church was finally reopened. The first Pontifical High Mass held in the chapel since the 16th century was sung by the Most Rev. Donald A. Campbell, D.D., Archbishop of Glasgow, while the Rev. Father David McRoberts preached the sermon.

The interior of the restored chapel (ill. 61) has a deliberately late medieval appearance — particularly in the case of the altar and painted altarpiece with cloth of gold frontal. The original baptismal font has been restored to use while the chancel screen and Rood Loft are in the old style. This Rood Loft displays the Great Rood with attendant figures of the Virgin Mary and St. John; in addition there are six coats of arms: those of Pope Paul II, Bishop Andrew Muirhead of Glasgow, and of Bishop George Lauder of Argyll (commemorating the 15th century consecration), and those of Pope Pius XII, Archbishop Donald Campbell of Glasgow, and of Bishop Kenneth Grant of Argyll and the Isles (commemorating the 1955 restoration). Underneath, linking the above two groups of shields is the coat of arms of Duncan Napier of Kilmahew.

For 23 years the chapel was served by priests from St. Peter's College at Kilmahew, but in November 1978 the tiny Roman Catholic parish of St. Mahew was created with Father O'Reilly the first resident parish priest presiding over a flock of some 120 people.

If you continue along the Darleith Road past Auchensail Farm you eventually enter lands once belonging to the estate of Darleith. Most of this estate together with the mansion house of Darleith lay within the parish of Bonhill and there is only space here merely to mention that the now sadly crumbling (and dangerous) old house of Darleith, home of the Yuilles from the 17th to the 19th century, has parts which date from the 16th century. Most of the building dates from later periods. Nearby stand a ruined private chapel with Yuille memorials, and a splendid old dovecot. Between Auchensail and Darleith there is a disused quarry which was worked during part of last century.

The old ruined Castle of Kilmahew is reached by following Barrs Road northwards and continuing past Kilmahew Farm. You turn right where the Cairniedrouth Farm road branches off to the left, and then walk south through a wood to reach the ancient ruin (ill. title page). This was the seat of the Napiers of Kilmahew from the 13th to the early 19th century. The building is in the form of an unpretentious tall keep of five storeys plus garret. This structure is probably partly 15th century and partly late 17th century with later windows and other alterations. Above the old north-west entrance is a wide lintel on which at one time was inscribed: "The peace of God be herein". Remains can be seen of a great fire-place, a turnpike stair, and a well. The interior is now all overgrown and damp and the ruin in a rather sorry state.

In 1820 the estate was sold by William Napier (heir of his uncle) whose sister Elizabeth had married a Mr. Sharp. This man's brother, Alexander Sharp, bought the estate and his children are recorded as having been born at Kilmahew between 1820 and 1828. Sharp had the castle altered somewhat to make it habitable — e.g., some new windows were built together with a new south-west entrance flanked with niches for columns. The number of storeys was reduced to three. However, the family resided latterly at Seabank, a house at the shore a few hundred yards west of Murrays Farm. By the time that James Burns had completed his purchase of the various parts of the estate of Kilmahew in 1859, the old castle was already in a semi-ruinous condition.

It has to be remembered that the one-time estate of Kilmahew included much of the land now occupied by Cardross village and that when the Burns family came to Cardross they were, in those days, coming as virtual feudal superiors of the community into a position of considerable local power and influence.

James Burns (1789-1871) was the first of Kilmahew. It was, however, his son John William Burns (1837-1900) who had the new mansion house of Kilmahew built. This splendid residence, begun in 1865 and completed in 1868, was designed by the celebrated John Burnet of Glasgow, and is situated a little lower down the hill from the old castle and on the opposite bank of the Kilmahew Burn. The situation is outstanding with glorious views over the Clyde towards the Renfrewshire and Argyllshire hills. Even Arran can be seen from the house on a clear day.

The mansion (ill. 62) is in the Scottish baronial style with Jacobean influences. The material used, a kind of grey freestone, was taken from a nearby ravine; while the various cornerstones were made from a lighter grey material brought from Glasgow. Altogether the house was built with three reception rooms, twenty-one bed and dressing rooms, a billiard room, and a library. There are some fine staircases and elegant wood panelling, and the house was famed for its collection of family portraits by some of the finest artists of the day. In the library there was a collection of some 5,000 rare books.

By 1891 the family was, of course, well established in the house and we can see from the census that present that night were four members of the family, two visitors, a retired nurse, and nine domestic servants. When we consider the number of gardeners, under-gardeners, foresters, gamekeepers, ostlers and stable boys who were also in the employ of the family, the total number must have been similar to some small-to-medium sized business today.

John William Burns was an advocate and a staunch Liberal, having been the candidate for the County seat on more than one occasion. He was also chairman of the Parochial Board and of the Parish Council of Cardross for a number of years, and was called upon to represent the interests of the village on countless occasions. In 1875 he acquired the additional estate of Cumbernauld in East Dumbaartonshire. His father and his uncle have an exalted place in Scottish shipping history, having founded the famous Cunard Company.

The gardens of Kilmahew were at one time the horticultural glory of the area, none but the best head gardeners being employed by the laird, and many were the visiting parties who enjoyed picnics there and pleasant walks along the wooded paths. John Fleming, gardener throughout much of the Victorian period, David Morris, gardener from towards the end of last century, and Frank Dunbar in more recent times (under the Allan family) were very eminent in their profession.

The estate of Kilmahew, which had been much augmented by the Burns family, amounted to 1,552 acres when it was sold in lots in 1919. It included the old castle, the mansion house and grounds, Asker Farm with Asker Hill rough pasture and plantation, Kilmahew Farm, Kilmahew Cottages, Low Milndovan Farm, Auchenfroe House and grounds with about an acre of woodland and a cottage, and Bloomhill House and grounds. The mansion house and grounds were bought by a wealthy Glasgow shipowner Claud A. Allan (1871-1945), of Messrs. R. & C. Allan. He had been residing in the house as tenant since 1908. His son, Commander Allan, succeeded in 1945 but the family left the area in 1948, and in that year the house and grounds were acquired by the Archdiocese of Glasgow for use as a Roman Catholic training college.

In connection with this establishment a new seminary was built adjacent to the house and inaugurated on 30th November 1966. This building, from designs by Gillespie, Kidd & Coia, received considerable acclaim in architectural circles. For its purpose it was designed with a main block containing a chapel, a refectory, and rooms for 102 students; and a detached block nearby with a library, communal and lecture rooms, and a convent for eight nuns.

Under the ownership of the Archdiocese of Glasgow, Kilmahew was usually referred to as St. Peter's College. This function ceased in 1976, however, and while various schemes have since been investigated for the buildings — from luxury hotel to a micro-chip technological research establishment(!) — the long-term future of both buildings, each noble and spectacular in its own way, is uncertain at the time of writing. For about a year now the premises have been used as a rehabilitation centre for people with drug addiction problems.

The influence of the estate of Kilmahew over the affairs of the village of Cardross has, of course, long since disappeared, together with a way of life the passing away of which some heartily welcome, some regret, but to which most are probably indifferent.

To the west of Cardross, opposite the entrance to the driveway of Geilston House, the Murrays Road branches off to the left. After a short distance an access road branches to the right towards Geilston Farm. The house called "Longbarn" can be seen amidst the trees, and a little further on stands the ancient but much-altered cottage called "Rosebank". Here the celebrated novelist A.J. Cronin was born on the 19th of July 1896. Cronin, however, only spent his very early years in this and in two other houses in Cardross before being brought up in Dumbarton.

There is a comparatively recent cottage at the next bend in the road. From here there is a long straight stretch leading via the Murrays railway crossing to the shore. On the left at the end of the road once stood a small cottage, probably originally occupied by a ferryman. On the right can be seen the old farmhouse of Murrays (ill. 64) which has undergone many alterations and periods of semi-collapse together with fire damage in recent times. Farm offices were at one time attached, occupied in Victorian years by agricultural labourers and their families. The farm was worked by the Sawmill McIntyres well into the present century, and by Bob Kelso under lease from them, but one has to go back in the records almost 100 years to find the last resident tenant farmer, John McFarlane, who died in 1885.

There was once a fishing yair at Murrays where a kind of dyke was built out into the river to trap the fish when the tide went out. This was one of a number of yairs along the Cardross shore, the most productive being in the west bay at Ardmore. It seems that the first "Comet" steamship may have called on one occasion at the Murrays Quay from Port Glasgow, and there is an old story that the Dixons of Dumbarton Glassworks had at one time considered the Murrays as a location for their premises.

This area is referred to as The Murrays, more correctly "Murraghs", meaning "grassy shoreland". A few hundred yards to the west once stood the house called "Seabank", the ruined remnants of which remained until only a few years ago. The shore path from The Murrays westwards can be followed as far as Ardmore.

The fields immediately north of The Murrays farmhouse were until recently a favourite with the target-shooting fraternity. This rifle range extended in olden days a considerable distance to the west and gave its name to a small cottage "The Butts" which once stood at a railway crossing below Moore Park, near a butt fifty feet broad by twenty feet high, behind the target. We are reminded that this area was used by the Cardross Volunteers for shooting practice and competitions.

The 7th (Cardross) Company of the Dumbarton Volunteer Rifles came into being late in 1859 largely as a result of the efforts of Major Joseph Tucker Geils of Geilston (1808-1871), who organised and persuaded, and arranged for funds to be raised to assist volunteers who could not afford to kit themselves out with the necessary uniforms and accoutrements. About thirty who were able to do so commenced drill before the end of 1859. The Rifle Corps was officially sworn in at the end of March 1860. Soon shooting competitions were arranged and at first a field at Carman was used; but when it could not be extended ground was secured near the shore here at Major Geils' expense in 1864. Major Geils was the commanding officer from 1859 till 1868 when he retired. He was succeeded by Lieutenant (later Major) Calder of the Colgrain Farm family, who in turn was succeeded by Captain W.B. Thomson in 1889.

The most famous member of the Company was, however, John McIntyre of the Cardross Sawmills, who, when an Ensign in 1870 was already recording victories in shooting competitions in England, Ireland, and Scotland. He was promoted to Lieutenant in 1870, Captain in 1880, and retired in 1887 with the rank of Major, having amassed a goodly number of trophies for outstanding performances all over the country, and having represented Scotland on many occasions.

Much excitement was caused in the area by two D.R.V. camps which were held at Ardmore in fields near Ardmore Farmhouse in July of 1889 and 1891. The fields were a sea of tents and marquees, with over 800 men present on both occasions. Drill sessions, inspections, shooting competitions, mock attacks, religious services, speeches, games and music, occurred. The men were well fed, receiving among other delicacies, three quarters of a pound of beef (without bone) every day, and there were plenty of opportunities for quenching thirst. "A couple of non-coms," wrote a Helensburgh journalist, "keep their eyes on the canteen to prevent illicit and immoderate drinking". By all accounts both camps were an enormous success.

The Cardross volunteers held an annual ball, an annual conversazione, and other events over the years. Many men in the village were involved and "volunteering" must have been the chief leisure interest of some. The Company employed a drill instructor who stayed in the flat at the Drill Hall.

Opposite the point where the Murrays Road leaves the main road an avenue leads northwards to Geilston House. Until very recently this avenue was lined with beautiful elm trees which were almost 200 years old.

The lands of Geilston have had a number of different owners: The Wood family in the 16th century, a branch of the Bontines in the 17th century, the Buchanans of Tullichewan in the earlier part and the Donalds of Lyleston for the rest of the 18th century and onwards until 1805. In that year the small estate was sold to General Thomas Geils of the Madras Artillery who had, in 1798, already bought the properties of Ardardan and Ardmore nearby. Before the General bought the house, however, it had been rented from the Donalds by Dr. John Moore of Glasgow whose son was later to become the famous Sir John Moore of Corunna. The story goes that as a small boy Sir John had nearly been drowned in the nearby Geilston Burn. The two mortars on the lawn in front of the house are reputed to have been used at his last battle.

General Geils settled Geilston on his second son, Colonel Thomas E. Geils who was succeeded by his brother Major Joseph Tucker Geils in 1845. Members of the Geils family continued to reside in the house until the early 1900s, but the venerable old building has been occupied by the Hendry family who came from Lennoxbank House in Balloch in 1910. James D.G. Hendry, who died in 1950, was the first occupant. His daughter is still resident.

The house (ill. 65) is in the form of an L-shaped range. A number of different periods and styles of architecture are represented, dating probably from the 17th century. The oldest part is shown at the far left of the photograph, while the newest 20th century part shown is the entrance porch at the single-storey extension at the right. Older parts of the house have many interesting low ceilings and sloping floors, and the interior is stylishly furnished. The grounds have often been open to the public for a day in summer as part of the Scottish Gardens Scheme.

There are many fine large houses in the vicinity of Cardross; but since this book is intended mainly to be a history of the village, there is only space here to make a brief mention of them. A few hundred yards west along the Helensburgh highway a narrow road goes off to the left to the houses of Ballymenoch, Brooks, Moore Park and Woodside. Ballymenoch is the oldest, an old farmhouse which has been altered over a period of time. The handsome Brooks house is definitely Georgian in appearance.

Woodside was built about 1862 for John Service, wholesale grocer, who prior to that had resided at the first Villafield house. John Macdonald (1844-1924) a well-known explorer in the Andes, Rocky Mountains, New Zealand, Australia, and the South Sea Islands, and one of the leaders of the gold rush to the Klondyke, was resident at Woodside for a time in the late 19th century. One of his sons, Alexander, a native of Cardross, founded the town of Cardross in North Queensland where he owned a copper mine.

Moore Park, built about 1864, was first occupied by Peter Wilson, wholesale grocer, (brother-in-law of John Service of Woodside), but from 1872 it was the residence of Dr. David Murray (1842-1928), a Glasgow writer and procurator, head of the firm of Maclay, Murray & Spens. He was probably the most learned man ever to have lived in Cardross. As well as being an acknowledged authority on many legal subjects within his own profession, particularly conveyancing, he was also a leading expert on archaeology, antiquities, and local history. In this last respect mention should be made of his book "Old Cardross" published in 1880, in which he concentrates on earlier centuries and on changes in land ownership and usage within the parish as a whole.

85

Dr. Murray had an enormous library of books many of which are now in a special collection in Glasgow University Library. Many of his books of local interest form part of the "Watchmeal Collection" at Dumbarton Public Library.

While Dr. Murray took a keen and active interest in many of the practical and cultural affairs of Cardross, one of his daughters, Eunice Murray (who has already been mentioned in these pages) was even more involved in the every-day activities of the area. She was active in the suffragette movement and even stood as a Parliamentary candidate for Bridgeton just after the First World War. She was a long-serving Dunbartonshire County Councillor and followed in her father's footsteps by writing about old Cardross. Two of her books, "The Church of Cardross and its Ministers", and a history of Cardross School, are standard works for any one studying the area in detail. In 1923 she was elected president of the Cardross Women's Rural Institute, the first "Rural" in Dunbartonshire. She died in March 1960. She and her sister Sylvia (who died in 1955) will be well remembered by some Cardross residents today. Our photograph (ill. 66) shows John Graham, chauffeur, standing beside the Murrays' family car, about 1914.

Still further west another road leads southwards to Ardardan. The old Offices are still there, but the house is new, having been erected shortly after the old house was sadly destroyed by fire in January 1977. This event was merely premature, however, as it had been intended to use fire anyway to assist the demolition which was in progress. The old house (ill. 67) was built in the 1770s for Andrew Buchanan, lessee. An eastern wing was added in the following century by a Mr. Claud Neilson, and further extensions were made in the later Victorian period. Beside the main road near the entrance to Ardardan still stand the ruined Ardardan Cottages with the Victorian villa "Tighmonadh" nearby, built 1878-9 for Thomas Campbell.

North of Mollandhu farmhouse stands the turreted baronial-style Drumhead House (ill. 68). The older portion behind dates from 1700, but the main building belongs to the next century. The Buchanan-Dunlop family owned house and estate for many decades, though the family of Campbell Martin (died 1948), an iron merchant, occupied the house from Victorian times well into this century. The house is now divided into flats. Drumhead, (or Badyen) Farm stands on the hill behind.

Past the entrance to Ardardan the peninsula of Ardmore can be seen on the left. Lyleston Cottage stands beside the road at the corner where one turns left into the Ardmore road. Lyleston Farm is near the top of this road and Ardmore Farm down near the railway crossing. The house on "Hill of Ardmore" dates from the beginning of last century and was built on the site of a previous building and there are some interesting ornamental and fortified features of uncertain date in the gardens which were probably laid out for General Geils. The house was mostly leased out during Victorian times. More recently it has been occupied by the Sloan Smith family.

If we return to the main road, Cardross Crematorium (opened in June 1960) can be seen to the north-east, and another road, "The Red Road", leads northwards towards the "Stoneymollan" and ultimately, via the farm of Blackthird, the vicinity of Balloch. Further west along the main road are the entrances to Lyleston House (ill. 69) and Keppoch House (ill. 70). Lyleston House and estate were long in the possession of the Donald family in the 18th and 19th centuries, one member of which, William Macalister Donald (d.1880) was Vice Consul at Ferrara in Italy. The house has had many different lessees and occupants since then, and is now divided into flats. The owner has built a new chalet-style house to the immediate west.

Keppoch House stands among fine trees a little west of Lyleston. It was built on the site of a previous house which was occupied by the Ewings of Keppoch in the 18th century, having taken the place of an old peel tower. The new house was built in 1820 for Alexander Dunlop, and was later occupied for some of the Victorian period by James Donaldson of Keppoch. Alexander Crum-Ewing of the Strathleven family was resident towards the end of the century, having bought the estate in 1882. The next occupant was Montagu M.W. Baird (1854-1915), chairman of Messrs. Hugh Baird & Sons, Ltd., maltsters and grain merchants in

Glasgow. In the dining room there is beautiful wooden panelling and a plaque is built into the wall with the following inscription: "This panelling was removed in 1904 from St. Anne's Church, Belfast (erected 1774). My parents Hugh Baird and Margaret Ferguson married in St. Anne's Church 17th June 1836 — Montagu M.W. Baird".

S. Crawford Hogarth bought the house in 1923 from Major Hugh Stanley Baird but the present owner is Mr. Brian McKinlay. The house has some magnificent carved ceilings and some idea of the splendour in which the before-mentioned Donaldsons lived can be gleaned from the sale of contents which took place in 1882. The items included (amongst countless others): mahogany dining room suite in crimson morocco, rosewood drawing room suites in silk damask and sewed work, Collard and Collard semi-grand piano in rosewood case, collection of favourite engravings in oak, rosewood, and gilt frames, library suite in walnut tree, bedroom furniture and fine bedding, hall furniture, etc., etc. Also sold were a family "bus", a landau, brougham, a phaeton, a carriage, farm horses, cows, queys, outdoor articles, etc., and the let of grass parks.

★ ★ ★ ★ ★ ★ ★ ★ ★ ★ ★ ★ ★ ★ ★ ★

## FARMING IN THE SURROUNDING DISTRICT

We have had occasion to mention farming a few times in the foregoing pages. Since Cardross was until recently a typical rural village, its connection with agriculture was, of course, considerable. Indeed, much of the area now built up was at one time farmland. However, there is no space here to go into details about the agricultural history of the area — that would be another book. A few comments are nevertheless appropriate.

Until the end of the 18th century most of the lairds concentrated their agricultural efforts on their Home farms. The outlying small farms (virtually crofts) were left much alone and little progress in methods of breeding or crop production had been made for centuries. In the era of "Improvement" which followed, however, the landowners began to invest more money and effort, and by the early 19th century in the Cardross area much had been done in the way of improved roads, enclosures, better farmsteadings, reclamation of waste land, drainage, and so on. Many cottaries and small farms disappeared, absorbed into bigger units. The tenant farmers became more sanguine about the changes when they saw the advantages. Payment of rent in "kind" gave way to money rents, and there were more modern preconditions (relating to performance) attached to the leases.

A local agricultural society was formed about 1839 and an annual ploughing match arranged which took place in January on a different farm each year. Competition was fierce and sometimes stirred the muse of one of the spectators. One, Robert Lawson, wrote concerning the 1869 ploughing match held at Craigend Farm then possessed by Hugh Urquhart:

CARDROSS PLOUGHING MATCH

Last Friday morn the Cardross lads they met to try their hand,
Down in a fine field of Craigend, at turning ower the land;
Fourteen ploughs came on the ground — their harness bright did shine —
The men and horses they were fresh, and started in good time.

Willie Traquair o' Cairneydrouth made twa fine rigs they say,
And carried aff the foremost prize frae Cardross lads that day;
A smart wee chap is James Traquair, his wark he made it tell,
And carried aff the second prize — the Cairney lads did well.

James Colquhoun of Kilmahew, he played his part gae weel;
The third prize he took hame that night, a sturdy clever chiel.
Next came a steady canty lad, and weel did haud the plough,
The fourth prize he did win that day — young John o' Kilmahew.

Johnnie Glen o' Wallacetown comes next upon the sod,
For his fine lot fifth prize he got — he made a bonnie job;
Next Jamie comes upon the ground among the Cardross men,
The hinmost prize was won by him, young Jackson o' Craigen'.

John McBride they did commend; the wark maun ha'e been gran',
For John's a tried and tested hand at turning ower the land.
Here's to a' the ither lads that nobly played their part,
They may ha'e better luck next year — they maun keep up their heart.

Here's to the Cairneys and the Glens, the boys o' Kilmahew,
And a' the ither Cardross lads long may they haud the plough.

From the 1850s onwards, threshing machines were being tried out on some Cardross farms — the new technology of the period. Many farm servants and agricultural labourers were employed for short spells by the farming families. These servants lived in bothies or farm "offices", or in the village itself. As farming gradually became more sophisticated with the development of machinery of greater efficiency, the industry became less labour intensive. Farmers in the area are now much more independent and some are owner occupiers. From the middle of this century the connection with village life has declined.

We have two fine farming photographs: the first (ill. 71) shows harvesting at Lyleston Farm in the early years of this century; the second (ill. 72) is a splendid view of Lower Auchensail Farm about the same period. It is worth recording that The Very Rev. John Anderson Graham (1861-1942) of Kalimpong, Bengal, the famous missionary who was also Moderator of the General Assembly of the Church of Scotland, spent his early boyhood at Auchensail where his father was a farmer.

Wallacetown Farm, as well as being one of the fine thriving farms in the immediate vicinity of the village of Cardross, also has, it is interesting to note, a curious place in the history of aviation, for it was from one of its fields that Percy Sinclair Pilcher (1867-1899) experimented with three different gliders between 1893 and 1896. In 1894 he had been appointed assistant lecturer in naval architecture and marine engineering at Glasgow University. He soon after became interested in power flight and it is likely that had it not been for his untimely death by accident while demonstrating a superior glider at Stamford Hall, Market Harborough, on 30th September 1899, he would have made considerable progress. Wallacetown Farm might have been a place of historical pilgrimage for historians of aviation!

## THE PLACE-NAME "CARDROSS"

The name "Cardross" has given rise to a certain amount of etymological controversy. It is generally agreed, however, that the "-ross" part (Old Gaelic "ros" = "promontory") derives from the sloping tongue of land stretching from Clerkhill or Kirktonhill to Sandpoint opposite Dumbarton Castle. It should be remembered that the name refers to the parish and that the parish church was at Kirkton of Levengrove in ancient times.

David Murray's view was that the first syllable of the word comes from Gaelic "Cathair" meaning "fort" and he argues that there must have been some fortified place in that area at one time.

John Irving (who was not a Gaelic scholar) gives two meanings in his "Place names of Dumbartonshire" (1928): (1) Gaelic "Caer ross" = "the point on the moorish ridge"; (2) Gaelic "Car rois" = "the curved point". Another meaning suggested by some is "rowan tree promontory".

Ian McKinnon, a former Cardross schoolmaster, argued that the meaning should be: Old Gaelic "Cardden" = "copse" or "thicket" + "ros" = "point" or "promontory". He pointed out that his view was supported by two important factors: firstly, the evidence of old forms of the name in medieval charters, e.g. Cadinros, Cardinros, Cardrose, Cardrois, etc. These suggest that the "d" in the name might not have been intrusive; secondly, he maintained that where an old Gaelic place name consists of substantive + adjective (in whatever order) the emphasis in pronunciation is almost always on the adjectival part. This being the case, a meaning such as "woody promontory" is possible, while "fort promontory" is nearly impossible. As all Cardross residents are aware the name is supposed to be pronounced with the emphasis on the first syllable. Ian McKinnon also pointed out that no remains of any fort have been found in the appropriate area, and there are no references to one in any records.

I myself am unable to add anything to these speculations except to suggest that if Ian McKinnon's views are accepted, the word "Cardden" looks very like a Gaelic version of an old Brythonic Celtic word. This old "British" language was spoken in the area over 1,000 years ago as the name "Dumbarton" ("fortress of the Britons") clearly testifies.

# SELECTIVE INDEX

ill. = illustration; ad. = advertisement

90

## OTHER DUMBARTON DISTRICT LIBRARIES PUBLICATIONS

Chirrey, James: The Loch Lomondside military road
Grant, Keith: The Skeets Gallacher story
Jones, Arthur F. and Hopner, Graham N.: The old Vale and the new
Jones, Arthur; Taylor, Michael; and Osborne, Brian: Transport: The Lennox albums I
Orton, Ian: The Dumbarton libraries 1881-1981
Osborne, Brian D. and Taylor, Michael C.: Discovering Dumbarton District
Osborne, Brian D.: Helensburgh and Garelochside in old pictures
Stott, Louis: Smollet's Scotland
Taylor, Michael C.: Dumbarton at work and play

JAMES RITCHIE,
BUILDER,
VILLAFIELD, CARDROSS.
BRANCH,   -   -   STRATHLEVEN PLACE, DUMBARTON.

Estimates given for all Classes of Work.
Jobbings Punctually attended to.

Old advert, date 1914

# JAMES RITCHIE & SON

## *Builders, Slaters and Plasterers*

◆

Houses to design with Modern Equipment and Labour-Saving Appliances.

◆

EASY FINANCIAL TERMS ARRANGED

**Jobbings a speciality.  Enquiries invited.**

PHONE CARDROSS 35

HOUSE - - **ENFIELD VILLA**
YARD - - **SMITHY ROAD**
**CARDROSS**

Old advert, date 1937